Annual Giving Primer

How to Boost Annual Giving Results, Even in A Down Economy

2010 EDITION

Scott C. Stevenson, Editor

WILEY

978-1-118-69197-7   ISBN

978-1-118-70406-6   ISBN (online)

2010 Edition —

Annual Giving Primer:
How to Boost Annual Giving Results,
Even in a Down Economy

Published by
Stevenson, Inc.
P.O. Box 4528 • Sioux City, Iowa • 51104
Phone 712.239.3010 • Fax 712.239.2166
www.stevensoninc.com

Annual Giving Primer: How to Boost Annual Giving Results, Even in a Down Economy

TABLE OF CONTENTS

Annual Giving Primer: How to Boost Annual Giving Results, Even in a Down Economy

TABLE OF CONTENTS

Annual Giving Primer: How to Boost Annual Giving Results, Even in a Down Economy

TURN TO CHALLENGE GIFTS TO BOLSTER GIFT INCOME

Challenge gifts can help boost annual giving efforts in multiple ways: 1) The challenge gift can add dollars to your annual fund — from the donor making the challenge — that might not otherwise have been realized; 2) the challenge can help to motivate both new and increased gifts from those who respond to the challenge; and 3) the added publicity your nonprofit can generate from a challenge gift provides added visibility for your organization and the annual fund.

Seek Out Opportunities to Establish Challenge Gifts

For those who may be new to the fundraising profession, challenge gifts are those in which one or more donors offer a sizeable gift if the institution can raise a specified amount of additional gifts from other donors over an agreed to period of time. The challenge gift can, in essence, be used to leverage additional gifts since donors are told their contributions will be matched.

It pays to seek out challenge gift opportunities. Consider the following options as you seek out challenge gift opportunities:

- **Board of Directors.** There are times when a board challenge can provide the impetus for others' giving. In fact, there are times when a challenge from one board member can motivate the remaining board members to contribute sacrificially.

- **Groups of individuals.** Sometimes it's difficult to raise the needed challenge from one source. If that's the case, consider a challenge made up of multiple donors.

- **Individuals.** Whether you consider approaching a new prospect or an existing donor for a challenge gift, know that this feature can be used to help leverage a major gift. The person's intended gift will receive a great deal of publicity and will help to encourage others to contribute.

- **Businesses and corporations.** Businesses often appreciate the visibility experienced as a result of a major gift. A challenge gift from a business would certainly bring about added visibility and would contribute to the business' image as an upstanding corporate leader.

- **Foundations.** Some foundations actually base their giving decisions based whether or not their grants would be used as challenges to leverage gifts from others. These foundations are often motivated to participate in projects that might not otherwise be successfully completed without their assistance.

Know What a Challenge Gift Should Accomplish

When establishing a challenge gift — a major gift given to a charity providing it is matched by gifts from others — how much thought goes into what you want it to accomplish?

Naturally, the challenge gift itself is a major achievement, but how you use that gift to leverage other gifts represents an important part of any challenge.

Do you want to use the challenge to generate new, first-time gifts? Do you want to use it as a way to encourage increased giving? Perhaps you are interested in generating more gifts at, say, the $1,000-plus level.

Before approaching a would-be donor for a major challenge gift, know what it is you want that challenge to accomplish.

Here are some ways you can use a challenge gift to leverage others' giving:

- A challenge aimed at a particular group — recent graduates, those residing in a particular city or state, members of a particular profession.

- A challenge matching only new and/or increased gifts over the previous year.

- One that matches donors who join a gift/membership club at a particular level during the course of the year.

- A general challenge that matches all gifts over a specified period of time. A challenge matching any gift often has a ceiling: "The Turner Foundation will match any gift throughout the current fiscal year up to $1,000 per donor."

- Those who have given first-time gifts and are being invited to give for a second year.

- Challenges directed to current and/or former board members.

- Those directed to employees — based on gift amount and/or percentage of employee participation.

- Multi-year challenges encouraging donors to also make a long-term commitment.

Challenge Gift Concepts

As you consider different types of challenge gifts and who you might approach to make them, give thought to an organization (a club or business) with many members or employees who, if your challenge is accepted, will get behind it and help you meet the goal.

One women's organization established a $250,000 challenge that would benefit a local nonprofit. Because all the club's members voted on whether to establish it, they all got behind it to see that the local nonprofit raised sufficient funds to qualify for the match.

Engaging the challenger's employees or members early on helps ensure they will get behind the effort and support it.

Challenge Gift Advice

- It's important to recognize that a challenge gift can motivate the challenger as much, sometimes more, as those expected to match the gift.

TURN TO CHALLENGE GIFTS TO BOLSTER GIFT INCOME

Challenge Can Generate Donations During Slumps

Gift challenges, growing in popularity among educational institutions, can be a successful way for all nonprofits to encourage giving.

Shaké Sulikyan, director, annual giving and alumnae relations, Pine Manor College (Chestnut Hill, MA), says a general participation challenge helped to more than double their number of monthly donors in May 2008. Here's how it worked:

As part of the college's fiscal year 2008 final push strategy, the college implemented the May Challenge. The goal was to get 200 donors in the month of May. If the goal was met, a donor had promised to give an additional $20,000. There were no restrictions on who the donors could be.

"An analysis showed that for each of the past five years, the only month we had more than 200 donors was December. Most months we have fewer than 100 donors, so this was a real stretch for us," says Sulikyan.

Sulikyan promoted the challenge through postcards sent out to all alumnae, parents and friends who had given to the college in one or more of the fiscal years 2005, 2006 and 2007, but had not yet given to the 2008 annual fund; an announcement in an alumnae e-newsletter and an e-mail sent to faculty and staff. A website, updated daily, tracked the progress of the challenge. Phone program callers mentioned the challenge during each call, which also helped with credit card donations. Finally, they sent out an e-mail to all non-donors four days before the deadline of the challenge letting them know they needed 43 more donors to reach the goal.

In the end, the college exceeded the goal with 245 donors giving a total of $59,391.

Source: Shaké Sulikyan, Director, Annual Giving and Alumnae Relations, Pine Manor College, Chestnut Hill, MA. Phone (617) 731-7099. E-mail: ssulikyan@hotmail.com

Trustees Drive Multimillion-dollar Challenge

Lawrence University (Appleton, WI) recently rolled out a three-year, $3 million challenge in hopes of gaining $6 million. And after the unexpectedly overwhelming success of a six-week blitz fundraiser, the Trustee Triple Treat Challenge (see box, below), organizers have no doubt they will meet that goal, says Stacy Mara, director of annual giving.

"We already had this challenge planned," Mara says, "but this is a collective trustee challenge rather than a challenge aimed at just a few individuals."

The goal of the challenge is to raise $3 million in funds, which will be matched, dollar for dollar, by the trustees who have already pledged $3 million in support over the next three years. Unlike their very successful Trustee Triple Treat Challenge, Mara notes that this fundraiser is also open to parents and friends of the school, as well as alumni.

Hopes are for the new challenge to draw donors who did not give in fiscal year '09 and those donors who have been at the same gifting level for several years, "Our experience has been that once donors reach a certain level, say $100 or $500, they get stuck. The idea here is to encourage them to move up to that next level," she says.

To do so, university staff are offering a dollar-for-dollar match to persons who did not give in fiscal year '09. For those who did donate, a match will be given when their fiscal year '10 donation allows them to move to the next giving level.

Donors can sign on to participate over the next three years, giving the university the ability to plan based on promised funds and donors the ability to see their gift doubled.

Advertising began in July with a Q-and-A article, The Economy, the College, and the Road That Lies Ahead, with Terry Franke, class of 1968 and Bob Anker, class of 1964 (www.lawrence.edu/news/pubs/lt/Summer09/Features/theeconomythecollege.shtml). In August, university staff released an e-mail video appeal to promote the trustee challenge. In September, class agents promoted the event in solicitation letters to classmates.

Source: Stacy J. Mara, Director of Annual Giving, Lawrence University, Appleton, WI. Phone (920) 832-6557. E-mail stacy.j.mara@lawrence.edu

Content not available in this edition

New Twist on Old Challenge Raises Nearly $1 Million in Six Weeks

In 2009, staff at Lawrence University (Appleton, WI) knew they needed a push to reach their funding goal. And so, the Trustee Triple Treat Challenge was born, wrapped in eye-catching pink flyers with a triple-scoop ice cream cone logo; a stretch for a university that is typically very traditional.

Stacy Mara, director of annual giving, says the idea came to her as she looked at trustee pledge commitments for fiscal year '09 and '10: "We were actually planning for a fiscal year '10 challenge and asking our trustees to make five-year pledges starting in fiscal year '10. Some of the trustees stepped up in fiscal year '09, so we decided that given our need... we'd use the fiscal year '09 trustee gifts and put forth the Trustee Triple Treat."

Stacy approached two trustees before presenting her idea to the campaign steering committee.

This challenge promised not just a match of alumni donations, but a double match, effectively tripling any alumni contribution. The result? An astounding $929,027 in funding.

Staff sent alumni an e-mail blast in May explaining the challenge and letting donors know they had through June to take part. They posted the challenge on the school's website and sent a mailing.

Mara says the challenge was open specifically to alumni, 1,147 of whom participated for a total of $309,676 in alumni funds. Add that to the $619,351 in matching contributions and Lawrence University raised nearly $1 million in six weeks.

TURN TO CHALLENGE GIFTS TO BOLSTER GIFT INCOME

Try a Group Challenge Gift

Challenge gifts are used all of the time to motivate others to give. Challenges include one-to-one matches, two-to-one matches, those that match all new and increased gifts and more.

For the most part, challenges generally come from one source — an individual, a foundation or a business.

Have you ever considered approaching a group of individuals to establish a challenge gift? Consider your board or better yet, a group of up-and-coming philanthropists who have or one day will have the ability to make a major gift.

In addition to motivating others to increase their giving, a challenge of this sort will have another important benefit: It will provide a meaningful way to involve this group of challengers in your advancement efforts.

Secure a Multi-year Challenge

Rather than a single year challenge gift, work at securing a multi-year challenge that can be used to match new and increased gifts over a three- to five-year period.

Multi-year challenge benefits include:

✓ Maximize the challenge gift.
✓ Leveraging new and increased gifts over a multi-year period.
✓ Building a yearly habit of giving among new contributors.

Timely Challenge Encourages New Donations

Creating loyalty in young donors can lead to bigger payoffs down the line.

Knowing this, Jamie Stack Leszczynski, associate director of annual giving, The Fund for Oswego (Oswego, NY), and development staff created a 10-year reunion challenge to not only celebrate alumni anniversaries, but engage them as donors.

Leszczynski secures volunteers from the class preparing to celebrate its 10-year reunion to serve as chairs of the challenge, helping create a goal and solicit classmates.

Classmates receive two mail solicitations challenging them to make a donation to help reach the goal in honor of their 10th reunion year. Volunteers also send e-mails and make phone calls to classmates.

The goal for the graduating class of 1998 was $10,000, playing off the 10-year reunion. By the end of the fiscal year, the school had secured 58 new donors, approximately 4 percent of the class, and raised $7,869. Matching gifts and pledge payments helped them reach their goal.

Class of 1999 volunteers are now challenging fellow graduates to not only reach the bar of giving $10,000, but to raise it. A letter to class members (shown at right) notes that if each class member gives just $19.99 they could raise $28,585.

Other changes to the Class of 1999 campaign include creation of a class website (e.g., "You know you attended Oswego from 1995-1999 when you remember…") and Facebook page, she says, noting, "We realized after the class of 1998 that if you focus on the 10-year class and give them a little more attention, the campaign will be successful."

She says this year's challenge is also focusing more on participation, with the hope that this push will re-engage those students who have lost contact. "Hopefully this will engage alumni who have not donated in the past, connecting them with the campus once again."

Source: Jamie Stack Leszczynski, Associate Director of Annual Giving, The Fund for Oswego, SUNY Oswego, Oswego, NY. Phone (315) 312-3121. E-mail: leszczyn@oswego.edu

This letter is an example of one of several pieces 10-year reunion members receive encouraging them to support an all-class fundraising effort for SUNY Oswego.

Content not available in this edition

TURN TO CHALLENGE GIFTS TO BOLSTER GIFT INCOME

Challenge Aims at Getting New, Increased Gifts

To continue to successfully raise funds in the current economic downturn requires creativity and innovation.

Early in 2009, members of the Stuhr Museum of the Prairie Pioneer and Foundation's development committee (Grand Island, NE) realized that because of the economy, soliciting gifts for the museum's annual fund could be especially challenging.

So instead of asking their loyal donors to increase their gifts in the tough economic times, they decided to target new or renewed donors.

The goal of the foundation's A Time Like No Other... campaign was to attract 550 new or increased donors in 2009, a 16 percent increase (75 donors) over the 2008 campaign, which attracted 475 donors. The dollar goal remains the same as 2008: $180,000.

Giving early momentum to the effort, an anonymous donor also pledged a $15,000 challenge match for new donors. (New donors are defined as those who have never contributed to the museum's annual fund and renewed donors are defined as lapsed donors who have not contributed for at least one year.)

The campaign kicked off in March with a closing date of mid-July. Gifts normally continue to come in beyond mid-July, and are still credited to the campaign through Dec. 31 of the campaign year, says Pam L. Price, the foundation's executive director.

"We typically end up quite a bit over the public goal," she says. "For instance, in 2008, we announced on July 17 that we had reached (and surpassed at 107 percent) our fundraising goal of $180,000, raising $193,370 from 442 donors. By Dec. 31, we had raised $203,363 from 475 donors."

In May 2009 they had raised $139,714 in gifts and pledges from 379 donors. They had attracted a total of 97 new and renewed donors (40 new and 56 renewed). At the same time the previous year they had raised $159,877 from 379 donors.

"Since we had the exact number of donors — 379 — that we had at the same time last year but had raised $20,000 less, this reinforced our decision to target new and renewed donors and use the A Time Like No Other... theme for our 2009 campaign," Price says.

Twenty-two of 2009's new and renewed donors came on board as a direct result of the progressive strolls that take place in Stuhr Museum's recreated 1890s Living History Railroad Town, says Price. She notes that the events have also helped bring in 17 new memberships to the museum in 2009.

> **Challenge Gift Idea**
>
> To reach first-time donors and nurture annual giving, have someone establish a challenge gift that matches first-timers' initial and repeat gifts over three years.

The strolls, which make people aware of the museum and its programs, include an ask, says Price. "While those making the ask explained the foundation would mail campaign materials within the next two to three days, we also had pledge cards and membership materials on hand."

When the campaign ended in July 2009 the museum had by far reached its goal. They had obtained 168 new donors and raised $191,955.

Source: Pamela L. Price, Executive Director, Stuhr Museum Foundation, Grand Island, NE. Phone (308) 385-5131. E-mail: pprice@stuhrmuseum.org

Challenge Hopes to Increase Recent Graduate Participation

To increase participation by recent graduates, officials with Hamline University (St. Paul, MN) launched a month-long challenge to nondonors who graduated between 1997 and 2007.

Molly Bass, assistant director, annual giving programs, says that during a brainstorming session with colleagues and the alumni annual fund board of directors, they reached a consensus of the importance of getting recent graduates on board financially. So they took action.

"With nearly one-third of graduates from the last decade making up our alumni base, we recognized that this group is an incredible resource with great potential," says Bass. "In many ways they are the future of the university. Getting this group involved in Hamline, through volunteer work or financial support, will influence how much we are able to grow."

Karla Williams, director of annual giving, presented the idea of the Gold Challenge to the alumni annual fund board. The board, in turn, agreed to match dollar for dollar any gift of $10 or more made by nondonors March 1 to 31.

To market the challenge, university staff created a series of five e-cards and two postcards. The university's call center also dialed this group for three weeks, while class agents from 1997 through 2007 sent personal e-mails and postcards to the target group.

"We knew we had to be creative and responsive with this group," says Bass. "Graduates for the last 10 years desire and expect more than traditional fundraising pieces. They like choices and want to be able to easily make their gifts online and this series of five e-cards — one every Tuesday during March — gave them the ability to direct their gift to an area that matters to them."

The challenge resulted in more than 60 new donors and more than $2,500 raised (before matching funds). Bass notes that it was interesting to find out that in terms of distance, the closest gift came from her office — a young alumna who works in alumni relations — and the gift from the greatest distance came from Brussels. Both gifts were made online.

Source: Molly Bass, Assistant Director, Annual Giving Programs, Hamline University, St. Paul, MN. Phone (651) 523-2787. E-mail: mbass01@hamline.edu

TURN TO CHALLENGE GIFTS TO BOLSTER GIFT INCOME

Client Challenge Creates Opportunity for Annual Campaign

How can you challenge your donors to add more funds to your annual campaign?

When a young client brought a homemade apple pie to radio personalities running the annual radiothon for the Make-A-Wish Foundation® of the Mid-South (Memphis, TN), she had no idea how much support she would end up generating for the campaign.

Off the cuff, the personalities posed a challenge: What if the young chef — a youngster who had her wish granted by the nonprofit — sold her homemade pies for $500 a piece? The child took that challenge and easily sold more than 20 pies.

The pie challenge has become a regular part of the campaign, with approximately 10 pies being sold, raising enough money to grant the wish of a child every year.

Source: Liz Larkin, President/CEO, Make-A-Wish Foundation of the Mid-South, Memphis, TN. Phone (901) 680-9474. E-mail: llarkin@midsouth.wish.org

Challenge Gifts Help Increase Number of Annual Donors

The 2007-2008 school year began with a trustees challenge for parents of students who attend Washington Episcopal School (Bethesda, MD). And if school officials and annual giving volunteer leadership got 100 percent of parents to make a gift by the 100th day of school, the trustees would donate an additional $25,000 to the school.

They made that goal — with three days to spare.

The purpose of the challenge was to reach the school's annual fund giving goal of $350,000, an increase of 18 percent over the previous year, according to Claire Henderson, assistant director of development.

"To meet the challenge, we decided we needed to formulate a plan of action to increase annual giving participation and increase gift size," says Henderson.

To do so, school officials launched a full-scale campaign that included:

- Encouraging everyone to give 20 percent more than their previous year's gift.

- Mailing solicitation letters to parents regarding the importance of annual giving for the school.

- Following up letters with a phonathon by class representatives.

- Sending e-mails and making phone call reminders of the 100 percent participation goal.

- Mailing end-of-year postcard reminders urging parents to give.

- Publishing class giving participation rates in the school's newsletter to encourage those who had not given to participate.

- Mailing an annual report draft listing contributors names to encourage last-minute gifts.

Henderson says the school's hard-hitting tactics worked, achieving the participation goal on Feb. 7 (three school days before the challenge was scheduled to conclude) and raising $377,000 to date.

Source: Claire Henderson, Assistant Director of Development, Washington Episcopal School, Bethesda, MD. Phone (301) 652-7878, ext. 212. E-mail: chenderson@w-e-s.org

Trustee's Challenge Statistics

To measure the success of the Trustee's Challenge for Washington Episcopal School (Bethesda, MD), look at the statistics:

✓ In 2006-2007, 33 percent of the parent body gave 20 percent more than the previous year; in 2007-2008, 38 percent gave at this level.

✓ All eight of the returning families who did not give in 2006-2007, did give the next year.

✓ In the 2007-2008 school year, the school had 100 percent giving participation by new families (37) compared with 91 percent of new families (45) the previous year.

✓ In 2006-2007, the school saw 70 percent parent participation by mid-February; the next year, it reached 100 percent. At the end of 2006-2007 the school saw a 93 percent parent participation rate.

✓ Parents gave $10,000 more in 2007-2008 compared to the previous year, despite having 16 fewer families. Average parent gift size: $1,206.

✓ Of the school's 232 families, 19 percent were new annual giving donors in 2007-2008.

Challenge Gift Errors to Avoid

Challenge gifts can provide powerful benefits if used judiciously. But some organizations turn to challenge gifts haphazardly, and that's a mistake.

Avoid these challenge gift blunders:

- **Having challenge gifts too often.** Donors will become immune to challenges if you have them too often.

- **Challenges that are too complex.** Some challenges are set up with so many matching restrictions — what counts, what doesn't, or to whom the challenge applies — that people ignore them. Try to keep it simple.

- **Concurrent challenges.** Challenges going on at the same time will impede, even confuse, people's motivation to give.

- **Challenges that don't appear genuine.** Many challenge gifts are set up so the donor agrees to make his/her gift even if the match fails to be met. That's wrong.

- **Turning to too many donors for one challenge** — If you can't establish a generous challenge gift by going to one or a few sources, it may come across as meaningless to those being asked to match the challenge: "Why should we match a challenge gift that took 30 people to establish?"

TURN TO CHALLENGE GIFTS TO BOLSTER GIFT INCOME

Approach $1,000-plus Prospects With Challenge Options

As you begin a new fiscal year and you're approaching $1,000-plus contributors for support, why not add some leverage to your ask by inviting them to establish a challenge gift at a higher level?

Since there are any number of challenge types you could put forth, approach several of your past donors and $1,000-plus hopefuls with a menu of challenge concepts from which they can choose. After all, the more you engage a prospect in discussing and identifying a challenge gift opportunity that is appealing to him/her, the more likely he/she is to step up to the plate and establish a challenge gift. Think about it: Wouldn't you have a wonderful problem if three different people or businesses agreed to establish three different types of challenge gifts for your annual fund?

Perhaps one challenge would be to match any first-time gifts of $25 or more. Another might be to match any current and former board members who increase their giving by $500 or more. And a third donor could create a challenge gift that will match any current donors who increase this year's gift by 10 percent or more.

You have nothing to lose and everything to gain by exploring challenge gift ideas with your more generous donors and capable prospects. Any challenge gifts leverage others' giving and also can motivate the challenger as well.

Challenge Gift Concepts to Consider

Here's a small sampling of challenge gift concepts you could share with potential challengers. Match —

✓ All new and increased annual gifts.

✓ All board members (current and/or past) who increase their gifts.

✓ Past contributors who gave under $100 but choose to give at that level or higher this year.

✓ All businesses making a first-time contribution.

✓ Anyone who increases their level of annual support to $1,000 and any first-time $1,000 contributors.

✓ Any lybunt or sybunt who gets back on board as a current contributor.

✓ Anyone who moves from one giving club level to the next higher level.

Keep the Challenger Up to date on Matching Gift Progress

Whenever you're fortunate enough to have a donor put up sufficient funds to establish a challenge gift, it's important to keep the donor informed throughout the challenge period. In addition to just being a good stewardship practice, doing so increases the odds of the challenger adding to his/her pledge or repeating it sometime.

Whether your periodic updates include correspondence, phone calls, personal visits or a combination of each, provide an ongoing printed report — such as the example to the right — that the challenger can use to get a quick read on the status of matching gifts. The frequency of updates should be based on the duration of the challenge period. If, for instance, the challenge covers a three-year period, quarterly updates might be appropriate. You may also choose to let the challenger decide how often he/she would like to review updates, and issue them accordingly.

Challenge Gift Update
PREPARED ESPECIALLY FOR ALFRED M. WILSON
Jan. 4, 2010

Challenge Start Date _____Jan. 1, 2009_____ End Date ___Dec. 31, 2011___

Challenge Rules: Dollar-for-dollar match up to $1 million throughout the three-year period. Any gift directed to this project will be counted as a matching gift.

Use of Challenger's Gift: To establish The Wilson Leadership Symposium, an annual event that brings together some of America's top entrepreneurs who will publicly address key issues that impact the free enterprise system.

Use of Matching Gifts: All matching gifts will be directed to The Wilson Leadership Symposium Endowed Fund.

	Year 1	Year 2	Year 3
	Amount/No. Donors	Amount/No. Donors	Amount/No. Donors
Apr	$ 14,000 / 16		
Jul	$ 48,000 / 37		
Oct	$ 66,500 / 44		
Dec	$ 89,000 / 43		
Total	$ 217,500/ 140		

TRIED-AND-TESTED RETENTION EFFORTS

Knowing it's far easier and more cost effective to retain a past donor than to convert a non-donor, especially during a down economy, it's particularly wise to identify and focus on retention strategies that will ensure a high percentage of past donors will continue their support of your organization each year. In addition to traditional retention strategies, identify new and improved ways of ensuring that past contributors will at least repeat their level of support.

Track Who Is Giving How Much Throughout the Year

Whether your fiscal year ends in June, July, December or some other month, it's helpful to track who has given — and who has not — throughout the year. By breaking donors and prospects into categories, you can better evaluate what fundraising strategies to focus on throughout the year.

Use the form below (or develop one of your own) to analyze who is giving on a month-by-month basis. Donor/prospect categories for this example include:

1. **Repeat donors** — Those who gave last year and have given again during the current year.
2. **Increased donors** — Those who gave last year and contributed even more this year.
3. **Decreased donors** — Those who gave less than their previous year's gift.
4. **First-time donors** — Those who have either never contributed or have not done so in the past five years.
5. **Lybunts** — Those who contributed last year but have not done so this year.
6. **Sybunts** — Those who have contributed some years (within the past five years) but have not done so this year.

Using the example below, you can see that while certain donor/prospect categories are up over a year ago (i.e. repeat and increased donors), others are down. Total giving to date reflects a decrease of $6,500 in overall giving. One of many conclusions that can be made from this report indicates that there are 69 lybunts who contributed $11,000 last year and still might do so before the end of the current fiscal year.

Content not available in this edition

Track Last Year's Contributors' Current Year Giving

Sounds simple, but you'd be surprised by the number of development shops that don't track their last fiscal year's contributors. Whether you have a computer program that will do it, or it's done manually, develop a report that lists, alphabetically, every one of last fiscal year's donors along with their gift amount and the current year's target amount. Then, as you proceed through the year, periodically mark everyone who's been solicited and has given to date. This helps to better visualize where you're at in gift retention and helps prevent past contributors from falling through the cracks.

Your periodic gift report may look something like this.

2008-09 Donor Retention Report				
2007-08 Contributors	07/08 Amount	08/09 Target	08/09 Actual	Comments
Abbas, Richard	$150	$200	$200	Fall Phonathon
Acme Printing	$400	$500	$500	Personal Call: 8/08
Anthony, Susan	$250	$300		Community Campaign
Bedell, Richard/Emily	$75	$100	$75	Fall Phonathon
Bosco Pharmacy	$250	$300		Community Campaign
Byron, Noel	$1,000	$1,500		Personal Call: 11/08

TRIED-AND-TESTED RETENTION EFFORTS

Keys to Retaining Donors

Given the steady decline in donor retention rates this decade (fortunately per capita gift amounts are going up), and a growing lack of confidence in nonprofit organizations, what can charities do — or do more of — to retain their donor base?

"It's an easy fix," says John Taylor, principal, Advancement Solutions Consulting Group (Durham, NC). "Communicate in the right way, with the right information, with the right frequency."

Taylor suggests the following:

1. **Make sure expectations are clear and documented up front.** Your pledge/gift/endowment agreements should articulate what form the communication will take, its frequency and roughly when the donor should expect it. Any deviations from the documented plan should be communicated with the donor in advance.

2. **Communicate with your donors in the manner they prefer.** For some, a standard activity report may suffice. For others, especially if the gift amounts are large, detailed summaries of income and expenditures are routine. Still others may prefer the more personal approach — hand-delivery of a summary report coupled with an informed discussion of the program they have funded and plans for the future. This option is a critical step if you are considering a subsequent solicitation.

3. **Follow up with donors 30 to 60 days after you provide information.** Unless donors specifically request no phone calls from your institution, a simple call to inquire if they have received the information and whether they have any questions is suggested.

Many organizations suffer from lack of coordination when communicating with donors, Taylor says. "It is amazing how many donors are turned away ... simply because they did not realize they were bombarding donors with solicitations and appeals from every corner. Make sure you know who your donor wants to hear from, and in what frequency. That's a key to retaining donors."

Source: John Taylor, Principal, Advancement Solutions, Durham, NC. Website: www.advancement-solutions.com

Help First-time Donors Feel a Part of the Family

New gifts don't always come easily. And when they do materialize, it's important that your first-time donors know they are now a part of your organizational family. This is especially critical as you work to build a habit of repeat giving.

Stewardship procedures for first-time contributors should be distinct from others. These examples illustrate steps you might take to encourage those initial gifts:

1. List and welcome new contributors in your regularly published newsletter or magazine.

2. Host a quarterly reception or open house or tour of your facility, especially for all first-time donors.

3. Provide a membership card or special lapel pin or some other item signifying the contributor's official entrance into your charity's membership or family.

4. Offer an invitation or discount to a series of your scheduled events throughout the upcoming year.

5. Form a stewardship committee whose job it is to aid first-time contributors or members in becoming familiar with the organization and its programs and services.

Identify Strategies for Retaining First-time Donors

Once you've had the good fortune of generating high numbers of first-time donors, it's important to teach them the habit of repeat giving. Getting a second gift — even if it's a year later — is key to building a repeat donor.

That's why it's important to identify strategies to bring about a second gift within a year's time. Follow these methods to generate second gifts from first-time donors:

1. **Introduce your organization properly.** Remember, you may have received a gift for reasons other than their belief in your mission. They may have simply attended a special event or sent a memorial gift. It's up to you to introduce your organization to them and justify a repeat gift down the road.

2. **Steward the donors appropriately.** Incorporate steps throughout the year to show your appreciation and demonstrate how their gifts are making a difference. Consider special recognition — such as a paid ad in the local newspaper, or a special listing of new contributors in your newsletter or magazine — that impresses your gratitude upon them.

3. **Create multiple links between the donor and your institution.** Explore and offer various ways for these first-time donors to become involved. Ask board members or others to express appreciation for these persons' gifts, through personal notes, phone calls or one-on-one gestures.

4. **Tie future gifts to projects that interest them.** Because these first-time donors may have had no previous affiliation with your cause, match their interests with projects that will more readily merit another gift.

5. **Make them feel like part of the family.** As each week and month goes by, take cultivation steps to make them feel a part of your cause and constituency.

TRIED-AND-TESTED RETENTION EFFORTS

Monthly Giving Program Proves Mutually Rewarding

Development staff at Stonehill College (Easton, MA) make giving easy for donors in an effort that also saves the college money.

The Catholic college offers a monthly giving program allowing donors to make an annual contribution of $100, $250, $500 or $1,000 in 12 payments. For some, the smaller payments, ranging from $8.34 per month to $83.34 per month, are more manageable, says Lisa Richards, director of the annual fund.

"If they have always given $500 per year but that is too much out of their budget to do it all at once, making monthly payments of $41.67 is easier," Richards says. "Some are able to maintain their giving level this way; others have increased."

From Stonehill's perspective, the program also is cost effective.

"The monthly giving program allows us to count them as a donor right away, and we stay in good contact with them," Richards says. "We remove them from solicitations throughout the year, helping us save on mailing costs."

To participate, donors complete the monthly giving program enrollment form, designating an amount they want charged to their credit card each month. Stonehill's development assistant enters the gifts monthly. Donors receive an acknowledgement letter that indicates the donor will receive an annual summary statement report af-ter Dec. 31. The report details each monthly transaction and serves as a receipt for the calendar year.

In fiscal year 2008, only one year after its debut, approximately 90 donors contributed $18,000 through the monthly giving program.

To implement a similar program, Richards recommends the following:

❑ Plan everything from direct marketing pieces to data entry to acknowledgement letters and receipts.

❑ Be prepared to follow up with donors whose credit cards expire or do not process.

❑ Develop a plan to send donors a yearly statement and receipt for taxes if you do not acknowledge/receipt each monthly transaction.

❑ Think how this program can be an incentive to the donor to give (and hopefully give more) and explain how these gifts help the institution.

Source: Lisa Richards, Director of the Annual Fund, Stonehill College, Easton, MA. Phone (508) 565-1341. E-mail: lrichards@stonehill.edu

Be Assertive About Re-establishing Ties With Lybunts

How much time and attention do you put into lybunts — those who gave last year but not this year?

The most many organizations do with this group is to send multiple appeals with the hope of getting these past supporters back on board as donors. But it pays to do more than that, particularly if the lybunts are higher-end donors giving, say, $500 or above.

Don't just send lybunts direct mail. Be more proactive than that. Meet with them to find out what's going on in their lives and their work. Get a handle on their current perceptions of your organization and programs. Ask them for advice. Share opportunities for involvement along with opportunities for contributions.

You no doubt know there is a far greater cost of time and money associated with acquiring new donors as opposed to retaining former ones. That's why it's important to have a plan of action for lybunts that involves more than increased direct mail requests.

Rules of Thumb

When contacting lybunts — those who gave last year but not this year — turn to the rule of thirds: one third will give again, one third will consider a repeat gift and one third will refuse your request.

Double Up on Retaining Current Donors

During tough economic times, it's especially important to do all you can to retain past contributors. Evaluate past retention strategies with an eye on what more you can cost-effectively do. Examples of retention strategies may include:

• Contacting past donors early in the fiscal year rather than waiting until the gift anniversary.

• Increasing the number of face-to-face contacts (rather than direct mail or phone) as a way to convey the importance of gift continuation.

• Maximizing pledge payment options (monthly payments, credit card payments, electronic funds transfer) to make giving as painless as possible for your donors.

• Establishing a challenge gift aimed at past donors to leverage their ongoing support.

TRIED-AND-TESTED RETENTION EFFORTS

Carefully Craft Messages To Persuade Lapsed Donors

Do you direct targeted appeals to lapsed donors to get them back on board?

Here are some phrases to get you started creating the most suitable and effective message for your audience:

- Your support continues to mean so much to us. May we count on you again this year?
- We've missed your participation. Please join us for another year.
- I don't know any other way to say it: If your support isn't there this year, we won't be able to....
- We take great pride in having your name associated with our agency. I hope we can count on your participation again this year.
- I was reviewing our list of contributors to date and noticed your name was missing. So I'm calling you to share this friendly reminder.
- We have exciting news! We can break a new record in gift support this year, but only if past contributors continue to invest in our effort. Can we count on you for a gift of....?

Lybunts May Require an Extra Incentive

Lybunts — those who gave last year but not this (year) — sometimes require a bit more motivation to get back on board with an annual gift. So rather than push your needs ("We need your gift to meet this year's goal"), make an offer with them in mind.

Consider these and other incentives to convince lybunts to make a current year gift:

1. **Funding choices.** Rather than asking for a general gift, give them some funding options to choose from.
2. **Premiums.** Get a limited edition of something donated (photo, watercolor) that will be distributed to all current year donors as a keepsake. Or kick it up a notch by awarding donated items based on the size of gift given, such as those awarded by public radio and TV stations.
3. **Social opportunities.** Announce a donor-only event to be held at the end of your fiscal year, something with drawing-card appeal: a performance by a well-recognized entertainer, the presence of a celebrity, etc.

Help Sybunts Become Regular Contributors

What are you doing to actively convert sybunts — those who give some years but not every year — into habitual, yearly donors?

Time spent to make regular donors of this group is probably more cost- and time-effective than simply trying to acquire new donors each year, so it makes sense to have a plan for converting them into regular contributors.

Include these and other ideas as methods for helping them establish a regular habit of giving to your organization:

- **Identify all of your sybunts.** Review your database to cull out all sybunts, including the dates of their most recent gifts and the appeals to which they responded (i.e. direct mail, telesolicitation, etc.).
- **Categorize those names by the amounts that were given by each donor, then devise a plan to approach each category of names.** Example: Those who gave $500 or more receive a personal call if within a 200-mile radius. Those outside of the radius receive a phone call from the president of

your organization. Those who gave $100 or more receive a personal visit, if possible, or a phone call at minimum. Those who contributed $100 or less receive up to a series of three personalized direct mail appeals.

- **Provide a variety of restricted gift opportunities that will appeal to sybunts' interests.** In reviewing your list of sybunt donors, you might discover that they have only given when their gift was directed to a particular project or program. Rather than asking this group for unrestricted gifts, provide them with choices. You may, in fact, choose to offer the higher-level donors with much more personalized giving choices while offering lower-end donors with a standardized menu of choices from which to choose.

You may discover, after identifying all sybunts from your database for the past three to five years, that this pool of sometimes-contributors represents a tremendous potential for yearly support of your cause.

Procedure Follows Anniversary of Previous Year's Gift

There are many ways to get repeat gifts from a previous year's contributors. Whatever procedure you follow, it's important to have a system in place for re-securing those gifts. Here's one such procedure:

1. Contact the previous year's contributors 10 months after their last gift, reminding them what they did previously and inviting them to increase their level of support.
2. Have a method of contact to be followed depending on their level of past support. For instance, you may want a personalized letter for anyone who gave less than $500; a

personal phone call for those who gave $500 to $999, and a face-to-face visit for all $1,000-plus contributors. This is a simplified version what might normally be more sophisticated but does illustrate the concept.

3. In addition to the type of approach taken depending on level of past support, you will want a series of follow-up procedures for gifts that don't matriculate after a certain time. For instance, with those who received a letter but have not responded after 30 days, a personal phone call may be the next step; and so forth.

TRIED-AND-TESTED RETENTION EFFORTS

Phrases for Lapsed Donors

When crafting an appeal letter targeted to lybunts — those who gave last year but not this — here are some phrases to help get the creative juices flowing:

✓ We're so grateful for what you have done in past years. That's why we were sorry to have missed your gift this past year.

✓ We really don't want to lose you, [Name].

✓ We need your support now more than ever.

✓ We treasure your friendship and hope we can count on you to remain a supporter.

✓ "Things happen." That's what we told ourselves last year when your gift didn't show up. But this is a new year, and we really need your help.

✓ I honestly can't imagine what it would be like not having you as a friend of our agency.

> **Donor Retention Tip**
>
> ■ Send all of last year's donors a renewal invitation at the beginning of your fiscal year offering a special incentive for everyone who contributes 10 percent more than last year within so many days of receiving your appeal.

✓ Last year's annual honor roll of contributors just wasn't complete without your name appearing on it....

Proactive Tactics Boost Fulfillment Rate

What steps are you taking to increase annual fund pledge fulfillment rates?

Lee MacVaugh, a professional fundraiser who works for a Washington, DC nonprofit, shares ways his office has increased its pledge fulfillment success rate by nearly 25 percent in three years:

1. **Extending challenges.** The first challenge was made by the chairman emeritus of the board to the community to match, one for one, every dollar received above $200,000, while another proposal to the board chairman asked him to donate $50,000 once the office exceeded 75 percent support from those who pledged at the beginning of the fiscal year. MacVaugh says both these challenges were vital to increasing his office's success rate.

> **Help Fulfillment Rate**
>
> To increase your year-end pledge fulfillment rate among higher-end donors (annual gift donors with pledges of $1,000-plus), ask board members to accompany you on personal calls throughout the last quarter of your fiscal year.

2. **Staying in front of the donor all year.** Whether it's inviting donors to local/regional events, sending a special mailing after implementing a successful program or attaching personal notes to newspaper articles, each communication is tied back to the pledge. MacVaugh says they also use communication tactics (e.g., website, blog, newsletters, direct mail reminders) offering donors reminders to fulfill their pledges.

3. **Asking board members to call/meet with high-end donors who have yet to fulfill.** Volunteers call the $50 and $100 pledges.

4. **Including a notice in the annual report.** "This has been a spur to giving and fulfillment," says MacVaugh. "The first year we chose to publish the total yearly dollar figures and the percentage of givers helped us increase our fulfillment by more than 20 percent."

5. **Listing the programs/projects that need funding.** Each quarter MacVaugh lists these programs/projects in need of funding and reminds donors how their pledge can help the organization achieve its mission and expand its reach.

Source: Lee MacVaugh, Professional Fundraiser, Washington, DC. Phone (202) 296-7743, ext. 14. E-mail: lmacVaugh@character.org

Increase Your Pledge Fulfillment Rate

What percentage of your pledges goes unfulfilled from year to year? More importantly, what are you doing to decrease the number of unfulfilled pledges?

Here are some suggestions on how to address that problem:

• Emphasize the payment period when the pledge is accepted.

• Publicize a special premium for all donors who pay prior to your fiscal year end.

• Make personal calls on higher-end pledges prior to your fiscal year end.

• Send periodic reminders to those who made pledges.

• Direct a personalized letter (under your CEO's or board chair's signature) to unpaid pledge donors in the final days of your fiscal year.

• Launch a phoning effort to unpaid pledge donors in the final days of your fiscal year.

• Offer ample payment options: credit card, monthly/quarterly billing, online payments, electronic funds transfer (EFT), automatic payroll deduction and more.

TRIED-AND-TESTED RETENTION EFFORTS

Think Creatively to Encourage Donors To Send Payments

Looking for inspiration to encourage pledge payments? Here are two ideas to consider:

✓ **Handwritten notes** — For three years, mailed pledge reminders from Marist School (Atlanta, GA) have included handwritten notes from the school principal reminding donors of the importance of fulfilling pledges to the school's annual fund and thanking them for their continued support. In 2008, the school sent 330 reminders with the note and received 163 pledge payments. "It is a personal touch and our donors are very responsive to that kind of contact," says Katie Reilly, database administrator.

✓ **Recorded phone reminders** — Gillette Children's Foundation (St. Paul, MN) blasts automated calls to all donors with unful-

filled pledges. The blasts are recorded using a hardware/software package contracted from a telemarketing company and delivered via auto dialer. Messages are typically delivered by the CEO or other leadership staff, says Andrew Olsen, senior annual giving officer. The call is a simple reminder message to mail in their pledge forms or go online and make an immediate credit card gift. When tested in 2008, they saw a lift of about 7 percent in year-end response rates, and received fewer than a handful of complaints, says Olsen.

Sources: Katie Reilly, Database Administrator, Marist School, Atlanta, GA. Phone (770) 936-2226. E-mail: reillyk@marist.com
Andrew Olsen, Senior Annual Giving Officer, Gillette Children's Foundation, St. Paul, MN. Phone (651) 229-1766.
E-mail: aolsen@gillettechildrens.com

Get Those Pledges Paid Up

As you approach the end of a fiscal year, you can bet some donors will need an extra nudge to get their pledges paid up.

Making personal calls is particularly important for you and your staff to do with persons who have made higher-end pledges (e.g., $1,000 and above, depending on your organization and overall donor profile).

Instead of stressing the importance of meeting your year-end goal, emphasize the impact their gift will have on your organization and those you serve. For example:

Solicitor: *"Dan, we're so grateful for your pledge and are counting on you to come through prior to June 30, our fiscal year end, to be sure we can offer as many scholarships as possible to deserving students. Could we possibly get your check today?"*

Although the donor may or may not choose to send a check by year-end, it makes good sense to extend an invitation to fulfill the obligation while you're meeting with him/her.

GIFT CLUBS AND OTHER WAYS TO UPGRADE DONORS' GIVING

Beyond retaining donors, identify and pursue fundraising strategies that will help to increase donors' level of support. Gift clubs provide ways to encourage increased annual giving. Analyze your gift clubs (or levels) to be sure they are accomplishing what you want them to achieve. Does each club offer an appropriate gift range and accompanying benefits? Do the benefits become more exclusive and inviting as you move to each higher gift club? Are the names of each club appropriate? To what degree are you involving volunteers in each of your gift clubs — as a way to recognize donors and recruit others to become members of each club?

Analyze Year's Worth of Giving by Levels, Clubs

How much attention do you pay to gift results as they relate to giving levels or clubs? Analyzing those results annually can help identify ways to enhance your organization's fundraising strategies (see analysis graph, shown to the right).

Knowing each level's total donors, gift amount and how gifts were solicited can help you to make more informed decisions regarding future fundraising strategies.

If, for instance, you see significant growth in a particular level or club, you may choose to focus more fundraising strategies on that level. Or if a club is not living up to expectations, you may decide it's time to revamp its benefits or take other actions.

2009 GIVING BASED ON CLUB LEVELS

Club/ Group	Gift Range	No. Donors/ % of Total	Total Gifts	% of Total Dollars	Direct Mail	Tele-solicitation	Personal Calls
J. Doe Club	$5,000-plus	18 (2%)	$147,000	44.0%	None	1 (5.5%)	17 (94.4%)
Gold Circle	$1,000-4,999	34 (4%)	78,500	23.6%	6 (17.6%)	2 (5.8%)	26 (76.4%)
Benefactors	$500-999	65 (7.6%)	41,200	12.4%	12 (18.4%)	4 (6.1%)	49 (75.3%)
Patrons	$100-499	218 (25.5%)	38,900	11.7%	171 (78.4%)	41 (18.8%)	6 (2.7%)
Friends	Up to $99	517 (60.7%)	25,850	7.8%	344 (66.5%)	156 (30%)	17 (3.3%)
		852	$331,450		533	204	115

Put Some Thought Into Your Gift Club Names, Benefits

When was the last time you evaluated the various giving levels or clubs and accompanying benefits you offer to those donors who contribute varying amounts?

What you call each gift level and what you offer as corresponding benefits are no trivial matters. Granted, many persons will give based on other reasons, but if your gift clubs (or levels) influence even 5 percent of your constituents, isn't that reason enough to evaluate this aspect of your development operation?

In evaluating your gift clubs and corresponding benefits, ask these key questions:

1. **Should the names of each giving level or club be changed?** Make the names of giving levels distinctive to your organization's mission and history. Don't fall into the common century club label for those who give at the $100 level, for

instance. Be creative. If that's difficult, consult a reputable ad agency for ideas or sponsor a contest to name the gift clubs.

2. **Should the gift range of each level be changed?** Analyze how many gifts you have been receiving at each level. Perhaps you have too many lower-end categories.

3. **Are the benefits offered for each giving level conducive to increasing support?** If you intend to offer benefits, make them meaningful. Even more importantly, distinguish benefits between each level to make upgrading support more compelling.

4. **How does the prestige of the top giving level stand apart from all lower levels?** The benefits and distinction of your top giving level should be the envy of donors at lesser levels. All constituents should perceive membership at this level to be imposing.

Renaming Your Gift Clubs?

Whether you're starting from scratch or reevaluating your charity's gift clubs or giving levels, put some thought into naming each club. The names you select for each level should possess a certain panache and connection to one another.

To help you select from a variety of gift club names, consider these possibilities:

- Club names that convey integrity: Ambassadors, Distinguished Fellows, Diplomats.

- Names that convey perpetuity: Legacy Fellowship, Heritage Society.

- Nationally historic names or dates — The 1776 Society, The Order of Martin Luther King.

- Elements or objects akin to your organization's mission — an environmental organization might select tree-related elements: The Acorn Club, The Mighty Oak Guild, etc.

- Physical attributes of your facilities: Eternal Fountain Alliance, Order of the Chimes, Rose Garden Society.

- Notable individuals from your organization's past (e.g., employees, founders, board members and more — The Susan Monroe Society).

- Endearing names: Angels for Children, Lifesavers Club.

- Names tied to traditions (i.e., mascots, school colors and more: The Blue and Gold Club, Tiger Loyalists).

GIFT CLUBS AND OTHER WAYS TO UPGRADE DONORS' GIVING

Look at Sharing Benefits With Another Nonprofit

What sorts of benefits do you offer donors at each gift level? What if you could double those benefits?

Consider the possibility of partnering with another dissimilar nonprofit to share benefits for donors who give at a particular level each year. What would you have to lose?

Imagine a college, for instance, partnering with a local art center. Any donor who gives $500 or more during the year — to either charity — would qualify for benefits at each

organization. So if a donor gave $500 to the college, she/he would not only receive certain benefits from the college, but from the art center as well.

Explore the possibilities. The collaborative effort may attract and retain more donors.

Gift Club Tip

■ To give each of your gift clubs the attention they deserve, appoint a committee to each club and charge them with responsibility for recruiting, retaining and recognizing donors at that level.

Set Yearly Gift Club Goals

As you set your yearly fundraising goal, get specific. Set goals for each giving level or gift club. How many new $1,000 gifts do you intend to secure for that giving level? By what percentage will contributions to your $100 to $250 gift level increase next year?

Breaking down a yearly fundraising goal helps define specific actions you will need to take to achieve it.

Upgrade Donors With a Simple Ask

Just ask. Can upgrading donors really be as simple as that? It is for Ohio Wesleyan University (Delaware, OH).

"We believe here at Ohio Wesleyan that you have to just ask," says Mayme Norman, director of annual giving. "Our donors upgrade because we ask them to, and we provide a variety of methods to give."

Norman cites three ways in which university staff and volunteers ask for support:

- **Involving callers with a vested interest:** "Our student callers are very aggressive in asking for upgrades because we teach them that the cost of providing education continues to rise, causing the need for more support."

- **Providing direction, opportunity to increase prior gift:** "Through our direct mail campaign this fiscal year, we gave each donor their three-year giving history along with an elevated ask structure in order to increase their gift."

- **Empowering those making face-to-face asks:** "Knowing that personal contact with donors is the best way to increase gifts, we equip each development officer with the tools needed to ask for upgraded annual fund gifts, along with their capital and estate gift requests."

Using these techniques Ohio Wesleyan is 11 percent ahead of its annual fund goal compared to this time last year.

"The philosophy that the relationship drives the gift has worked very well for Ohio Wesleyan," Norman says. "We appreciate and promote relationship management when it relates to our top donors."

This elevated ask structure — personalized with a donor's giving history and proposed gift increases that are based on that history — helps Ohio Wesleyan University raise annual funds.

Content not available in this edition

Content not available in this edition

Source: Mayme Norman, Director of Annual Giving, Ohio Wesleyan University, Delaware, OH. Phone (740) 368-3302. E-mail: mhnorman@owu.edu. Website: www.owu.edu

GIFT CLUBS AND OTHER WAYS TO UPGRADE DONORS' GIVING

Create Giving Categories That Speak to Donors' Hearts

Boost your annual giving campaign by creating giving options that let donors follow their passions.

Doug Gortner, principal, Wessebago Consultancy (Nashville, TN), suggests setting up several distinct funds rather than one general fund. For instance, a school could ask parents to contribute to the function(s) that involve their children: Soccer parents would give to the soccer fund; theater parents would give to the theater fund, etc.

"Folks can give where their passion lies," Gortner says, "but you wouldn't be doing the duplicitous 'check the box where you want your gift applied,' knowing full well that the contributions are fungible and go into one big pot."

Offer motivation to further drive funds and staff buy-in, he says: "A key incentive would be that if gifts to a specific area exceeded budgeted expenses, those monies could be used by that sector for other legitimate expenses, such as new violins, new uniforms, new test tubes, etc."

However, he notes, an organization must be prepared to use general revenues for funds that fall short of their giving goals.

Although this alternative to a single-fund annual campaign may be more labor intensive, he says, the results are worth it.

"The donors would have an affinity to the area they are supporting, hence would be more likely to give generously and get actively involved in solicitation," Gortner says. "The rationale for fundraising would be apparent, as opposed to a commonly held attitude that the annual fund is a black hole or that you are asking for money just to ask for money. "

Source: Doug Gortner, Principal, Wessebago Consultancy, Nashville, TN. Phone (615) 730-7825. E-mail: wesebago@sover.net

---

Creating Giving Categories

To establish categories within your general fund that pull at donors' hearts, Doug Gortner, principal, Wessebago Consultancy (Nashville, TN), advises:

- Establish a database capable of creating standardized reports well ahead of time.

- Survey your constituents to determine their reaction using focus groups, paper questionnaires, online surveys or interviews.

- Begin small with a modest pilot program.

- Conduct a silent campaign. Publicize its results. Before announcing the new option to give to several funds, ask key donors for leadership gifts. If a particular fund does not produce one, ask insiders to lead the way.

- Thoroughly educate constituents. "This sort of change is rife with the possibility of misinterpretation and the resulting rumors," Gortner says. To bypass this, offer a one-hour forum for employees and donors. Allow 30 minutes for questions and answers.

- Have fun, knowing that successful fundraising while stressful, is also joyous.

Giving Societies Create a Place for All Donors

Everyone knows that donor recognition is vital to donor retention. That is the motivation behind donor recognition efforts at the University of South Carolina (Columbia, SC).

"Colleges and universities should take the time to cultivate and steward donors," says Lola Mauer, director of annual giving. "Their gift is a testament to your institution and you want to ensure they remain loyal to your mission."

Offering no fewer than eight groups or societies for donors to belong to makes a statement about the appreciation the college has for its donors, Mauer says.

Some of the societies they have set up for specific groups of donors include:

✓ **Carolina Circle** — Honors donors who have made a gift for three consecutive years.

✓ **Carolina Guardian Society** — Honors donors of deferred gifts, such as trusts, bequests and annuities.

✓ **The Horseshoe Society** — Honors donors who have made cumulative gifts of $100,000 or more. There are four levels within the Horseshoe Society, based on various amounts of cumulative giving.

First-time donors receive a thank-you postcard introducing them to the Carolina Circle.

Eligibility for the various societies is based on annual, as well as cumulative giving, and includes corporate matches of individual gifts. These distinctions allow for inclusion into the highest annual recognition society for each donor.

With the donor recognition system in place, Mauer says, they are seeing first-time donations grow, more than 400 members in the Horseshoe Society and more than $14 million in matured planned gifts from the 564 members of the Carolina Guardian Society.

With donor recognition, Mauer emphasizes, the most important factor is not how you do it, but that you do it:

"Whether you recognize (donors) with a special thank-you call, a postcard or a note from a student, you're showing the investment that donor made is critical and creates opportunities for many people."

Source: Lola Mauer, Director of Annual Giving, University of South Carolina, Columbia, SC. Phone (803) 777-4092. E-mail: LMAUER@mailbox.sc.edu

GIFT CLUBS AND OTHER WAYS TO UPGRADE DONORS' GIVING

Annual Fund Donors Join Giving Circles

Annual fund donors at The Walters Art Museum (Baltimore, MD) receive more than a thank-you: They become members of the museum's annual giving circles. Donors contributing $250 or more join one of seven annual giving circles, each with unique benefits.

"Making people feel like they are valued and part of the spirit of a program is important," says Julia Keller, manager of individual and corporate giving circles.

To do so, the circles offer donors unique privileges outlined below:

Sustainer ($250 to $749):
✓ Invitation to one monthly reception and tour with museum leadership.
✓ Two single-use parking passes. Keller says the museum recognizes that parking is at a premium, so it awards annual donors free passes for a convenient parking space.
✓ Discounts on museum tours and events, as well as children's and family programs.
✓ Subscription to The Walters Magazine, published three times a year and featuring exclusive news about the museum.
✓ Reciprocal privileges at 30 select art museums across the United States.
✓ Discounts at local restaurants.
✓ A 10-percent savings in the museum's store and cafe.
✓ Recognition in the annual report.

Patron ($750 to $1,499)
✓ Sustainer benefits, plus an invitation for two to the Patrons Preview, allowing a private look at one of the museum's special exhibits before it opens to the public.

Curators' Circle ($1,500 to $2,499)
✓ Patron benefits, plus an invitation for two to the Curators Choice reception. Donors have the opportunity to hear in-depth discussions by the curators of current projects followed by cocktails in the museum's Sculpture Court.
✓ Donors receive four single-use parking passes.

✓ Special recognition on the Honor Wall, located in the lobby of the museum.

Directors' Circle ($2,500 to $4,999)
✓ Curators' Circle benefits plus invitation for two to the Director's Dinner, an annual dinner that gives donors a chance to dine with the museum's international board of directors and hear speakers from nationally recognized museums address current issues.

Henry and William Walters' Circle ($5,000 to $9,999)
✓ Directors' Circle benefits along with a private lunch and/or consultation with a curator or conservator.
✓ Invitation to join the Collectors' Circle Seminar Series. The four-part series affords donors the opportunity to attend an in-depth seminar by museum curators and conservators, with seminars presented in the original Walters' family parlor.

Founders' Circle ($10,000 to $24,999)
✓ Henry and William Walters' Circle benefits, plus a private dinner and tour for four with the museum's director.
✓ Invitation to join the Director's Travel Program and tour cities around the world with the chance to view some of the world's finest art collections.

Benefactor ($25,000 or more)
✓ Founders' Circle benefits, as well as a private dinner and tour for eight with the museum's director.

While several of the benefits were in place when Keller joined the museum staff in August 2005, she says she periodically reviews benefits to keep them current and is always looking out for incentives, such as ways to engage donors and give them more personal access to the museum.

Source: Julia Keller, Manager of Individual and Corporate Giving Circles, The Walters Art Museum, Baltimore, MD. Phone (410) 547-9000, ext. 314. E-mail: jkeller@thewalters.org

Four Ways to Move Donors to the Next Giving Level

As important as it is to retain existing donors year to year, it's equally important to have strategies in place upgrading past donors to the next levels of annual giving. Increased gifts from past donors can mean the difference between falling short of or surpassing your annual fund goal.

These principles will help you in the upgrading process:

1. **Clearly distinguish benefits at each donor level.** Publicize benefits associated with each of your organization's gift clubs or levels. Clearly distinguish benefits of each level to entice people to move up to the next level.

2. **Involve higher-end donors in upgrading those at lower levels.** Use donor peer pressure to convince others to join. Host prospective member receptions asking higher-level donors to invite lower-level donors.

3. **Make it easy (and painless) to increase one's gift.** Use credit cards, electronic funds transfers from donors' checking accounts, monthly envelopes and other methods to make increased giving as seamless and simple as possible.

4. **Allow donors to decide how their gifts will be used.** Invite existing donors to make a second annual gift — one that moves them to the next giving level — directed to a special project of their choosing. It's more appealing to contribute at higher levels when one has some say in how the gift will be used.

As donors increase their annual giving over time, they will be more prepared and likely to contribute even more significant gifts in the future.

GIFT CLUBS AND OTHER WAYS TO UPGRADE DONORS' GIVING

Society Gives Young Alums Stepping Stone to Major Gifts

Did you hear the one about the recent college graduate rolling in dough?

Neither did we.

Fact is, most recent grads don't have lots of money — some might not even have a job. So bringing these people into your donor fold takes patience and special care.

Carrie Moore, assistant director, donor relations, Texas Christian University (Fort Worth, TX), says their Junior Clark Society is one way they have found to engage young alums and help them move, slowly, up the ladder to major giving.

Based on the university's existing Clark Society, which gives special benefits to those pace-setting donors who make a gift of $1,000 or more, the Junior Clark Society uses a tiered system of giving to help build younger donors up to a major giving level.

In the first three years following graduation, Junior Clark members make an annual gift of $100. In years four through six, they make an annual gift of $300. Finally, in years seven through nine, they make an annual gift of $500.

The hope is that as their careers grow, so too will their incomes and the donations they are able to make to TCU. Ideally, by the time they hit year 10, annual giving will have become such a habit they will continue making gifts to the university.

For their participation, members receive an invitation to a Clark Society Weekend and other campus events, library privileges globally accessible via the Internet, recognition in TCU publications, a Junior Clark car decal and the opportunity to network with some of TCU's most successful alums.

Those who give $750 or more designated to the Frog Fan Club also receive a named, reserved parking space for TCU's home Horned Frog football games, and the university gets the chance to make lifelong donors out of some of the TCU's biggest fans.

The Junior Clark Society currently has approximately 250 members.

Source: Carrie Moore, Assistant Director, Donor Relations, Texas Christian University, Fort Worth, TX. Phone (817) 257-6965. E-mail: cmoore2@tcu.edu

---

High-end Annual Gifts: Bring Together $1,000-plus Donors

What benefits are you offering those loyal supporters who give $1,000 or more annually?

One such benefit should be an invitation to at least one special event celebrating their support while also drawing attention to the importance of giving at such a generous level.

Creating such an annual (or biannual or quarterly) event helps to convey your organization's recognition and appreciation of donors who give at that level. Equally important, it helps elevate the exclusivity of giving at these higher levels, motivating others to increase their giving to join the higher ranks.

Make Your Top Giving Level Meaningful

Most organizations have gift clubs categorizing annual gifts and recognizing donors at each level of support. It's particularly important to recognize annual donors at your top giving level. Why? Because providing special recognition to donors at the top level encourages those at lower levels to increase their contributions. In addition, increasing your pool of larger annual donors increases the number of prospects who can make even larger gifts when you launch a capital campaign.

While the majority of nonprofits recognize $1,000 or more as a major annual gift, you will need to target a top gift level that is appropriate for your organization. Consider the total number of donors you have presently and the percentage who annually contribute at each level.

Whether your top annual gift level is at $1,000 or $10,000 or $500, here are some ideas you can use to beef up the value of this important group:

- In addition to one brochure describing each of your gift clubs, design a special brochure for your top gift category. List the benefits of annual membership as well as the previous year's donors.
- Select a recognized and respected individual (or couple) to chair your top club each year. Utilize the chair's signature on special appeals and ask him/her to help host special events for this prestigious group.
- Select a name for the top club that sets it apart from the other giving level — The Society of..., The President's Guild, The Order of..., etc.

- Coordinate a special recognition event each year inducting new donors into the club or society.
- Host periodic receptions for the club throughout the year, some receptions might be for members only, while other might encourage members to bring prospective members as their guests.
- Present new contributors with a plaque which can have pieces added to it for each year they remain a donor at that level.
- Recognize donors at this level in a distinctive way in your annual report. Consider listing the number of consecutive years each donor has contributed (at this level) beside his/her name.
- Provide club members with invitations to special events held throughout the year.
- Ask club members to stand and be recognized at special events.
- Provide members with special parking privileges.
- All donors at this level should receive a personal note of thanks from the organization's CEO and/or chair of the club.
- Provide club participant with a regular letter from the CEO including insider information on the organization and its accomplishments.
- Invite club members to a board meeting to be formally recognized by your directors.

Making your top gift club special requires additional time and resources, but considering the payoff, it's well worth the effort. You'll have more annual donors giving at higher levels and more major gift prospects for your next campaign.

GIFT CLUBS AND OTHER WAYS TO UPGRADE DONORS' GIVING

Start a GOG Club For Most Loyal Givers

You've probably heard how board members should be expected to give or get sufficient levels of support to justify their participation on your board. That same concept can work to initiate a club of your most loyal constituents. You could call it the GOG Club (for give or get).

Those persons who join (not limited to board members) would be expected to either contribute at a certain level each year or find enough other contributors whose gifts will total that amount or more.

Let's say, for example, your GOG Club members are expected to each come up with $2,500 per year. That means they each pony up that amount or they solicit gifts totaling or exceeding $2,500 each year.

To continue to build a club of supporters at that level, ask for members' assistance in coming up with member benefits that will help motivate their participation.

Gift Club Tips

- When introducing a new gift club to your constituents, take the one-time opportunity to promote charter memberships: "Become a charter member of this new club and receive the following benefits..." or "Get in on the ground floor by becoming a charter member of this special club.

- If your organization doesn't have much history with giving clubs, start slow, then expand. Begin with one annual giving club, say at the $1,000-plus level, then add another club after you're sure about which direction you would go with them.

Test Gift Club Appeals

Try segmenting your prospect list by gift clubs. Then send an appeal targeting those within each gift club in an attempt to get them to increase their giving.

Take this approach a step further by sending out four different versions of your letter to a single gift club to test what letter pulls the best response from this particular group of givers.

Put Some Teeth Into Your Gift Club Through Sponsorships

Want to attract more $1,000-plus annual contributors? Maybe you need to bolster your top giving club to attract that level of giving.

Look to sponsors to underwrite particular costs that will help you identify, cultivate and steward donors at higher-end levels. Here are examples:

- Annual recognition banquet for $1,000-plus donors.
- Special thank-you mementos to recognize top donors (e.g., limited-edition photograph, paperweight, etc.).
- A classy honor roll of contributors booklet that showcases your top gift club and lists those who gave at that level during the past fiscal year.
- Food, refreshments and entertainment for quarterly members-only receptions.
- Appropriate gratuities (e.g., Christmas poinsettias, flowers at funerals, etc.) for upper-end donors.

If donors ever question how you can afford to provide so many perks for these more generous donors, you're able to point to the sponsors who underwrote those costs. Additionally, the sponsors know they are gaining visibility among your more affluent constituents.

Have You Considered a Club For All Sponsors?

You no doubt have special clubs for annual contributors who give at certain levels. Chances are you also have a special society for all planned gift donors.

But what about a club for all individuals and businesses sponsoring events and programs throughout the year? Why not bring even more attention to your sponsors by creating a special alliance catering to all sponsors for the current fiscal year? In addition to the more individualized perks you offer sponsors, a club such as this would allow for group-related functions and also help motivate others to become sponsors.

Create a Menu of Upgrading Approaches

How do you ask a past contributor for an increased gift? Do you have more than one approach? It makes sense to develop a menu of approaches from which to choose as you work to upgrade past donors' gifts.

Here are some examples to use as a guide in preparing your upgrade menu of asks based on:

Fiscal year goal — "This year's annual fund goal is 10 percent higher than what was raised last year. That's why we're asking everyone to consider a 10 percent increase in their giving."

Gift clubs — "You're only $50 shy of being included in the next-higher gift club. I want to invite you to be a part of that group."

Cost of providing services — "It's expected that the cost of providing the same level of services as last year will increase by 6 percent. If everyone can increase their giving by that amount or more, we can keep pace with what's been done in the past."

Additional projects — "I recognize and appreciate what you have already contributed this year, but it wouldn't be fair to you not to tell you about this special project that we're attempting to fund by year's end."

GIFT CLUBS AND OTHER WAYS TO UPGRADE DONORS' GIVING

Extra Project Gives Justification for Increased Gifts

Looking for ways to get annual contributors to increase their level of support? Here's one approach that can help accomplish that aim:

1. Contact a past contributor and make the case for repeating whatever gift he/she made last year, then present a special project and ask for an additional restricted gift that will make that project a reality. For instance, say an individual has given $100 consistently for the past few years. This year you ask the donor to continue that important $100 contribution but, in addition, you ask for $50 more to support a special (and compelling) project that won't be realized unless everyone steps up to the plate.

2. Use this same approach for each of your giving clubs (or levels). For example, everyone who has given at the $100 level gets asked for an additional $50; those who traditionally give at the $250 level get asked for an additional $100 for your special project; and likewise for your other gift clubs.

3. You could have a different restricted gift project for each of your gift clubs, or you could have one major project. Try it one way one year and the other the second year. See what produces the best gift results.

Here's the point: Whatever approach you take, you're working at upgrading donor support and building a habit of increased giving.

Don't Be Shy About Asking for an Increased Gift

When approaching past donors for a gift, don't be reluctant about asking for an increase over the previous year. Just because economic news may be less than positive doesn't mean people are unwilling to give more. That decision should be the donor's, not yours.

Equally important, if you ask for more and don't receive it, you're in a stronger position to ask that the donor maintain his/her past level of support:

Solicitor: Last year you made a generous gift of $250 to our annual fund, and for that we are very grateful. I would like to invite you to contribute $300 this year.

Donor: I would like to, but with this economy, I can't justify doing that.

Solicitor: I can appreciate what you're saying. We will be grateful to simply have you maintain your past level of support this year. Can we count on you?

Donor: Yes, I can do that. Count me in!

Exercise for Increasing $1,000-plus Contributors

What role does a gift club or gift level play in motivating people to give to your organization? And when was the last time you evaluated your gift clubs to be sure they are accomplishing their intended purposes?

To get annual contributors to move up to your $1,000-and-above level, go to some of those donors in your next level down, perhaps donors at the $500 to $999 level. Set up a series of small group focus sessions with those at this level, say seven or eight to a group. Meet with each group and explain that you are attempting to make giving at the $1,000-and-above level a more meaningful and rewarding experience for those who give at that level. Point out the benefits of giving at that level, and offer some background regarding the makeup of that group. Then ask for those present to share their perceptions about that gift level — what appeals to them, what they are indifferent about and what they would change.

Although it may appear obvious that part of your rationale in bringing them together is to upgrade them to that higher level of annual giving, it should also be apparent that you have a legitimate reason for seeking their perceptions. Their input may, in fact, lead you to make some changes with your $1,000-plus giving club.

Why hold several small group sessions rather than one larger one? Three reasons:

1. People will be more willing to speak up and share when the group is more intimate.
2. Several focus groups allows you to do some testing to see what works best — asking different questions, holding each session in a different location, combining the work with social time to gauge what draws people to attend, etc.
3. If one member of a focus group becomes negative, the session will only impact a few rather than all of your $500 to $999 donors.

Develop a Repertoire of Increased Giving Pitches

Let's say your goal is to ask all existing contributors to increase their past year's gifts by 10 percent. How might you word that request? Although you will no doubt couch such an invitation in a more lengthy presentation, it would be helpful to have a menu of one-liners upon which to rely.

Here are some ways you might ask for a 10 percent increase:

1. If we can convince 80 percent of our donors to increase their annual support by 10 percent, we will surpass this year's goal.
2. Your $250 gift of last year was important to us and those we serve. To maintain our current level of services however, we are asking all contributors to increase their giving by 10 percent this year.
3. If it would be possible for you to increase your gift by 10 percent, you would become a member of our Pacesetters Club, which would include the following benefits....
4. I'm excited to share that we have a challenge gift in place whereby anyone who increases their giving by 10 percent or more will have their gifts matched by [Name of Challenger].

GIFT CLUBS AND OTHER WAYS TO UPGRADE DONORS' GIVING

Seven Ways to Upgrade Donors' Giving

How much effort are you putting into moving current donors giving levels up? In many instances, time spent doing that will be more productive than focusing on landing new gifts.

Incorporate these strategies for upgrading contributors' gifts:

1. Secure a challenge gift that matches all gift increases of $100 or more.

2. Approach current donors for a second gift before the end of your fiscal year.

3. Enlist the help of donors in a particular gift club to call on current donors giving at lower levels.

4. Identify a special funding project that will motivate donors to give more than in previous years.

5. Conduct focus groups to reevaluate each gift club's benefits.

Then publicize changes to all past contributors.

6. Emphasize quarterly and monthly pledge payments as a way to maximize giving.

7. Incorporate an annual fund theme that encourages increased giving: "7 Percent More Will Make a World of Difference!"

Upgrade Year-end Gifts

- Send a letter about a month before your fiscal year end to persons who have already made an annual fund gift. Tell them you're close to your goal and appreciate their gift. Then ask them to consider stretching a bit further to help you reach your goal.

Create Appeals Designed to Upgrade Donors' Gifts

How much planning do you put into getting existing donors to upgrade their giving from year to year? Mass appeals to an entire donor constituency just don't cut it anymore. It's important that you take a targeted approach in convincing donors to give more to your worthwhile cause this year than they did last year.

Experiment with these methods designed to upgrade donors' giving:

1. **Produce personalized appeals stating what the donor gave last year,** then ask for a specific increase.

2. **Develop a separate appeal letter for each of your giving levels or clubs.** If, for instance, you have a $100 to $250 level, craft an appeal that makes the case for contributing at the next higher level. In addition to pointing out donor benefits associated with that gift club or level, inform your audience that all gifts given at that level will be used for a specific — and appealing — purpose.

3. **Send a second or third appeal to current donors at midyear or during your fourth quarter,** pointing out what they have contributed thus far and let them know how much more they would need to give to move into the next donor level.

WORK TO BROADEN YOUR DONOR BASE AND RAISE MORE FIRST-TIME GIFTS

Just as it's important to focus your efforts on those who can give at more generous levels, it's also important to keep broadening the level of annual support. That's why some of your efforts should be directed toward acquisition of first-time donors. Although it may be more challenging to acquire first-time donors during tougher economic times, it's still wise to keep expanding your base of supporters. The strategies you employ to generate first-time gifts may be somewhat different than those you use for repeat donors. Equally important, once a non-donor makes that first-time gift, it's important to have strategies in place to cultivate the relationship and build a habit of giving.

Identify Ways to Generate Gifts, Reach First-time Donors

As important as major gifts are in the development process, it is also important to continue ways of generating new gifts from new donors. Here are 20 strategies to consider as ways to generate new gifts:

1. Ask your board to personally make a minimum number of new contacts over a specified period of time.
2. Approach people who use your services/programs and who don't currently give.
3. Ask current donors to invite a friend/associate to a get-to-know-us event.
4. Identify endowment gift opportunities.
5. Publish a wish list to distribute during personal calls, on your website and in printed communications.
6. Launch a buy-a-brick campaign that includes a brick engraved with donors' names.
7. Give volunteers credit toward prizes or raffle tickets for soliciting friends and family.
8. Set up an exhibit booth at fairs, malls and other locations to invite support.
9. Secure a challenge grant that will match new gifts.
10. Add family and friends of employees to your mailing list.
11. Get noncontributing businesses to sponsor an event, program or publication.
12. Identify non-donors on your mailing list and conduct a phonathon for a special funding project.
13. Make a staff commitment to make so many new prospect calls a week/month.
14. Begin a generational event (mother-daughter-grandmother) to invite family support.
15. Initiate brown-bag luncheons with a brief program and invitation to become a contributor.
16. Provide local service clubs with programs where you can share your wish list of gift opportunities.
17. Rent or exchange mailing lists.
18. Invite your constituents to organize a special event on your nonprofit's behalf.
19. Simplify the online giving process.
20. Begin testing e-appeals to select groups of names in your database.

Raise First-time Gifts in a Down Economy

Looking for ways to generate first-time gifts in a down economy? You can do so with a positive attitude and these strategies:

- Ask a loyal board member or major donor to establish a challenge gift that matches all new donors' gifts.
- Conduct a direct mail appeal to non-donors asking for small gifts for any compelling funding projects.
- Kick off a special fundraising effort among existing loyal donors: "Recruit a new friend for..." Then hold a party at the end of the effort inviting everyone who rose to the occasion, along with your new donors.
- Coordinate a special event. Anyone attending who's not already a donor becomes a first-time contributor.
- Meet with corporate decision makers and convince them to coordinate an in-house campaign encouraging their employees to support a particular project that won't get accomplished without their support.
- Share a list of fundraising projects for local civic groups from which current and potential donors can choose.
- Launch a new membership program that includes special benefits for anyone who joins.

Expand Your Donor Base by 20 Percent

What would it take to expand the number of current contributors by 20 percent? First, multiply the number of last fiscal year's contributors by 20 percent (1,000 donors times 20 percent equals 200.) Once you know that number, prepare an action plan identifying what your staff will need to do to generate your 20 percent.

Examples of action plan strategies might include:

✓ Send three additional appeal letters to prospects who are not currently in the database.
✓ Conduct a week-long phonathon directed to non-donors (or outsource the job to a telemarketing firm).
✓ Host a series of get-to-know-us receptions inviting individuals who have never made a contribution. Then follow it up with a solicitation.
✓ Coordinate a new special event aimed at attracting those with no prior history of giving to our organization.
✓ Launch a local campaign utilizing volunteers to approach new donors for first-time gifts.

WORK TO BROADEN YOUR DONOR BASE AND RAISE MORE FIRST-TIME GIFTS

Test Special Premiums to Boost Contributor Numbers

Are you looking to increase the number of annual contributors to your organization? Why not try some new approaches to see what works?

Do some test campaigns to limited numbers of nondonors, segmenting groups by certain criteria (i.e., age, sex, ZIP code, interests) and offering a particular premium if they make a contribution by a certain deadline.

Be fresh and creative in coming up with premiums that nondonors within a targeted group may find appealing. Partner with businesses and other organizations to be items or services donated for your special appeal.

For example, you might offer:

✓ A three-month complimentary membership at a cooperating fitness club for younger prospects.

✓ Participation in a special day-long field trip directed to retirees on your list.

✓ Free admission to a style show and lunch for women from more affluent ZIP codes.

✓ A free tree seedling families with newborns can plant in honor of the new baby.

Ask Current Donors to Spread the Word

To broaden your base of donor support, turn to existing donors.

Select a group of loyal donors and call them to let them know you appreciate their support and would like them to share their enthusiasm for your cause with three to five people in their circle of influence. Then, with their permission, mail them an envelope containing five appeal packages, along with a note explaining that they should hand-deliver or mail the packets to friends, relatives and associates and a deadline for doing so.

Each packet should include:

✓ A letter each individual can sign and personalize with a post script (see box, right).

✓ A short list of funding projects with associated gift amounts.

✓ Pledge cards, envelopes and return envelopes, plus information that lets would-be donors make gifts online if they so choose.

You may want to test this approach with a smaller segment of your donor base to measure its success and fine-tune it before launching it with more of your supporters.

When asking loyal donors to send information about your organization to colleagues, include a sample of a brief letter such as this for donors to personalize to include with the information.

[Personalize Salutation],

I'm personally asking you to consider supporting a cause I believe makes an important difference in our community — a cause that deserves far more support than it receives.

I regularly give financial support to [Name of Organization] because I can see the difference it makes in people's lives, too. The enclosure in this letter shares some of those valuable services and achievements.

I would be proud to bring you into the fold of loyal supporters. Please join me by funding one or more of the projects shown on the enclosed wish list. And please, do not hesitate to call me at [number] or e-mail me at [e-mail] if you have any questions about this organization and so I can tell you more about why [name of organization] deserves your support.

[Name]
[Personal P.S.]

Seven Ways to Promote Your Brick Campaign

Engraved brick campaigns are a great way to raise money for a specific project or program while beautifying an outdoor area. Here are seven ways to promote your brick campaign:

1. Include the campaign brochure in gift acknowledgments to donors who give to your annual fund or other programs.

2. Create a website specifically for promoting the brick campaign. Include information about where the money raised will go, how to purchase a brick, criteria for wording on the bricks, a map of where the bricks will be located, etc.

3. Send an e-mail solicitation to constituents for whom you have e-mail addresses, directing them to the brick campaign website for more information or to purchase a brick.

4. Create a traveling display for your brick campaign for external events, speaking engagements, etc.

5. Place ads about the campaign in your organization's newsletter, special donor publications and magazine.

6. Send a targeted mailing to memorial donors.

7. At the brick site, place a tasteful marker or notice stating the purpose of the engraved bricks, and whom to contact to purchase a brick.

WORK TO BROADEN YOUR DONOR BASE AND RAISE MORE FIRST-TIME GIFTS

Broaden Your Donor Base With Club of Like-thinkers

If you have a handful of like-minded individuals already committed to your cause — retired teachers, 20-somethings, professional women, stay-at-home moms, CPAs or fans of a sports team — consider helping them form a club. In addition to helping them connect, make new friends and enjoy camaraderie, you can also encourage them to work as a team to take on a funding or other project for the benefit of your charity.

Let's say you have a dozen 20-somethings who support your cause individually. Invite them all to form a club that meets monthly. Together, come up with a funding project the group can take on as their own. In addition to making personal gifts toward the project, part of their aim would be to enlist more members.

If 50 club members each contributed $100 each year for five years, they will have funded a $25,000 project.

Use this same model to start other clubs made up of various affinity groups. Over time, you can build a large and diverse base of involved donors.

Introductory Letter Helps Set the Stage

How can you go about making that first call on a new prospect?

Begin with a letter of introduction. It's professional, it provides a gentle way to break the ice and it helps set the stage for your eventual solicitation.

Keep your letter brief and make three basic points:

1. Explain how you got the prospect's name or why you decided to contact him/her.

2. Describe why the prospect should know about your organization. Point out ways in which your nonprofit benefits him/her directly or indirectly.

3. Briefly explain why and when you intend to call for an appointment.

Personalized Mailing Finds New Sponsors

While securing generous sponsorships requires one-on-one visits, direct mail can help to surface interested prospects.

Craft a personalized letter (and maybe a program or event summary sheet) to send to a large number of potential sponsors. Summarize sponsorship opportunities and point out the direct benefits of being a sponsor (publicity, free tickets, targeted exposure, etc.).

Include a bounce back form (see example at right) and return envelope inviting potential sponsors to express interest in learning more about sponsorship opportunities.

By directing a personalized mailing to a larger number of possible sponsors, you can attempt to surface those who have an interest in exploring sponsorships. This allows you to prioritize calls and avoids spinning your wheels contacting businesses and individuals with no interest in exploring sponsorship opportunities.

Sample bounce back used with letter to would-be sponsors.

Sponsorship Opportunities at XYZ Agency

Return this form to learn more about sponsorship opportunities and the benefits you can receive by becoming a sponsor. We'll contact you to set up a no-obligation, confidential appointment.

_____ Yes, I'd like to explore sponsorship opportunities.

_____ I'm particularly interested in the following sponsorship possibilities mentioned in your letter:

1. _____
2. _____
3. _____

Name _____ Title_____

Organization _____

Daytime Phone _____ E-mail _____

Commemorative Gifts Reach Out to New Donors

Since non-donors are more likely to donate toward something special, look for celebratory opportunities to invite support: your nonprofit's 10th, 25th or 50th anniversary, the retirement of your longtime CEO and so forth.

If you're celebrating an anniversary, for instance, invite gifts of $1 for each year your organization has been in existence, and direct those gifts toward a funding project that would appeal to first-time donors.

Choosing a funding project that attracts the community's attention and makes people feel good about giving (e.g., a healing garden or indoor aviary for the enjoyment of those persons you serve) can boost your chances for attracting fresh support.

Bolster Year-end Gifts

■ For any nonprofit that acquires books, offering donors the opportunity to have a book plate with a designated honoree's name on it — in exchange for a gift at a set minimum level — will help garner additional gifts and engage donors.

WORK TO BROADEN YOUR DONOR BASE AND RAISE MORE FIRST-TIME GIFTS

Make It Easy for Businesses to Solicit Their Employees

When people know what's expected of them, they're much more likely to pitch in and help. That's why you should make it easy for business owners and top management to invite their employees to support your charity. Here's what's involved:

1. Identify key business contacts who are already supportive of your organization — owners and top managers.

2. Develop a user-friendly packet of materials you can take to those individuals. It should include a simple outline of ways they can invite their employees to give to your organization, a sample script for the contact to put in a pitch when meeting with employees and sufficient brochures, pledge forms and return envelopes to be distributed to all employees.

3. Once you get one or two businesses that have successfully invited their employees to support your cause, bring those business heads along when you meet with and attempt to convince other businesses to participate. Ask them to give testimonials.

4. Identify perks tailored to these new business partners and any of their employees who make contributions.

Five Ways to Double Your Yearly Number of $100 Gifts

How many $100 gifts did your organization receive last year? What did those $100 gifts amount to collectively?

By knowing that information, you can set out to double the number of $100 gifts in the upcoming year. That doesn't mean you lessen the focus on generating major gifts; however, doubling the number of $100 donors not only brings in additional gift revenue but also helps to broaden your donor base. And the larger your pool of existing donors, the greater the likelihood of receiving more major gifts down the road.

Here are five strategies for doubling your pool of $100 donors in the upcoming year:

1. Analyze your $100 gift club or level and the accompanying benefits. Be sure donors are motivated to be a part of that gift club. Include some perks that are unique and special for members of that giving level.

2. Host a new $100-a-person special event — golf classic, fashion show, gala or wine and chocolate tasting — as a way to reach out to new donors and tell your organization's story.

3. Conduct a special phonathon effort asking prospects for $100 gifts to be used for a project donors will find appealing — plant a tree, establish a new scholarship, purchase a valued piece of equipment, etc.

4. Invite existing $100 donors to host small gatherings in their homes for the purpose of inviting guests to join them in contributing $100 to your cause. Use the gatherings as an opportunity to tell your story to attendees.

5. Convince a board member to establish a challenge gift of $100,000 to match all new gifts of $100 throughout the fiscal year. If successful, that's 1,000 new $100 gifts. (The board member's gift can be earmarked toward a specific project of interest to him/her.)

It's important to remember that having an ever-growing pool of annual contributors only improves the pool of potential major donors down the road.

Project Fundraisers Help Attract New Supporters

If your organization isn't in the midst of a capital campaign, now may be the perfect time to get one or more project fundraisers under way.

Much less comprehensive than a capital campaign, a project fundraiser identifies particular funding needs that are not part of the general operations budget yet are needed — a piece of equipment, supplies, funds for specific programs, for example.

For many would-be contributors, giving to a particular project is much more appealing than simply making an annual contribution that supports ongoing operations. Many colleges and universities, for example, get so caught up in asking for annual scholarship support that they miss specific funding opportunities that may have far greater appeal to potential donors. And seeking funds for a particular project doesn't have to be at the expense of asking for annual unrestricted gifts. Each have its place.

Advantages of Project Campaigns

If you're not currently in a capital campaign, make a point to have project campaigns in addition to your annual, unrestricted giving effort. Benefits to be realized include:

✓ Project campaigns can run concurrently with your annual fund effort.

✓ Your donor participation rate will increase by offering more gift options.

✓ More non-donors will begin to make first-time gifts.

✓ Existing contributors may increase their yearly giving by supporting both the annual fund and any of your restricted project campaigns.

✓ Your organization will realize some special needs that weren't a high enough priority for your general operations budget.

WORK TO BROADEN YOUR DONOR BASE AND RAISE MORE FIRST-TIME GIFTS

How to Secure Gifts From Surrounding Communities

It's often more challenging to secure gifts from surrounding communities even when your charity's services encompass their locale. And yet, the potential for broadening your donor base is worth pursuing every strategy available. Try any of these methods for reaching out to citizens in communities surrounding your nonprofit:

1. **Create community advisory boards.** Assemble individual groups of each community's movers and shakers to: a) make them aware of your charity's work, b) ask for their input in how you can be more effective in serving their community, c) seek their advice on how to raise local funds and d) invite them to serve as centers of influence on your behalf.

2. **Bring visibility to the ways in which your charity serves neighboring communities.** Hold an open house at your local branch office. Help shape feature stories for surrounding newspapers that illustrate outreach efforts.

3. **Earmark campaign funds for specific projects that benefit those communities.** People will give more willingly when they can see how their gifts are benefitting the quality of life in their own communities.

4. **Invite each community's leaders to become involved in fund development.** Ask community leaders to sign direct mail appeals for their respective towns. Invite them to chair and recruit volunteers for an annual community campaign.

5. **Establish a challenge gift for each community.** Go to an existing donor from each neighboring community and ask for a challenge gift that will encourage others to give.

12 Reasons Why $25 Gifts are Important

There has been so much emphasis placed on major gifts for so long that one begins to wonder if any effort should be put into securing smaller gifts, say for $25.

Clearly, every operational plan should include strategies directed toward securing such gifts. That doesn't mean time allocated to major gifts should take a back seat, but it does mean smaller gifts play an important role in the overall fundraising plan.

Here are 12 reasons why $25 gifts are important:

1. Most major gifts come from those who previously made smaller gifts.

2. Since word-of-mouth from a loyal donor is often a charity's best sales tool, it pays to have as many current donors as possible, regardless of gift size.

3. Converting 1,000 nondonors into $25 donors results in $25,000 in new gifts, an increase that most development offices would cherish.

4. A gift of $25 from a new prospect moves him/her into your membership or giving club pipeline. Benefits at each gift level should encourage him/her to increase giving over time.

5. Increasing the percentage of constituency giving — among your community, your employees, your alumni, etc. — provides a degree of leverage when approaching foundations for support. "Ninety-seven percent of our employees contribute and 77 percent of our community's businesses give annually."

6. Once someone contributes to your charity, he/she has identified him/herself as one who believes in and supports your work. You can then take steps to cultivate that relationship further.

7. Although there are many exceptions, most planned gifts result from those who have given previously.

8. Often the person who makes a smaller gift may be making more of a sacrificial gift (based on his/her income) than one who contributes at a higher level but could afford to do much more. And sacrificial donors — those who give to the best of their ability — are among your most loyal ambassadors.

9. Your published annual list of contributors serves as a testimonial to others who have yet to contribute.

10. Contributors often become involved in some volunteer capacity.

11. You cannot build a habit of giving without receiving that first gift, regardless of its size.

12. Both the donor and those served by the charity benefit whenever a gift of any size is made.

Major gifts — and the time devoted to their identification, research, cultivation, solicitation and stewardship — are important. But don't interpret that as a dictate to overlook approaches aimed at encouraging gifts at all levels.

TURN TO BOARD MEMBERS, VOLUNTEERS AND GROUPS FOR HELP

It's easy to write off going to board members and volunteers for fund development help. After all, it takes time to build a corps of committed volunteers. And there's no guarantee that the time you put into identifying recruiting, training and hand-holding volunteers will pay off. But if you make the time to do just that, it really will pay dividends. It's a long-term investment that requires more up-front time on your part, but it's worth it. Make it a priority to nurture board members and other volunteers. This chapter offers several ideas for doing that.

Ask Board Members to Commit to Fund Development Duties

If you fail to communicate expectations of board members to those board members, don't be surprised when they fail to meet those expectations.

To get board members to commit to helping your fundraising efforts, offer them a choice of three or four fund development options from which they can select. Then get them to commit to those choices.

At the start of a fiscal year or whenever a new board member signs on, share a fund development menu such as the example shown here. Explain what each involvement opportunity involves and then ask the board members to sign a commitment to follow through on whatever they chose.

As you prepare your menu of choices, you will need to decide what matters most: soliciting annual fund gifts, taking a leadership role in planning a special event, helping to identify and cultivate major and planned gifts, etc.

Board Fund Development Menu

As we enter a new fiscal year, please select two or more fund development responsibilities you are willing to undertake to help us achieve fundraising success during the next 12 months.

In addition to making a personal annual fund gift of $1,000 or more, I agree to help in the following two (or more) ways:

❏ *Annual Fund* — Identify and solicit no fewer than five donors capable of making President's Leadership Circle gifts ($1,000 or more).

❏ *Annual Fund* — Serve on the golf classic committee and enlist at least three foursomes ($250 per player) for the summer golf classic.

❏ *Annual Fund* — Serve on the business partners committee and strive to approach and solicit at least five new businesses capable of making gifts of $500 or more.

❏ *Major Gifts* — Serve on the major gifts committee and personally identify and cultivate two or more prospects capable of making $25,000 or more in pledges toward specific projects approved by the board.

❏ *Planned Gifts* — Serve on the planned gifts advisory council and work to identify and cultivate two or more individuals who possess the capability and proclivity to make a planned gift.

In accepting these responsibilities, I will provide the development office with updates on my progress on a quarterly basis throughout the current fiscal year.

_____   _____
Board Member   Date

Create Some Friendly Competition Among Board Members

Want to get your board more actively involved in fund development? Create a friendly competition to see who can make the most asks or raise the most in gifts.

Try it for a four-month period to test its effectiveness.

Pair up board members so they can make calls together, which is more fun than flying solo. Then divide the pairs into two teams. Give awards to the pair achieving the best results and an award to the overall winning team as well.

Awards need not be expensive. Think of what would most motivate board members: a dinner prepared by your CEO, a gift certificate to a great restaurant, having one of your programs named in their honor for one year or whatever strikes their fancy.

The ultimate goal is to get your board members more involved with and energized by raising funds.

Invest Board Members In Development Planning

You know that development planning leads directly to dollars raised, which supports the very existence of your organization. But how do you educate board members to make sure they feel the same way?

The following tips can help:

✓ **Include a specific developmental planning component.** Of course you need to revisit the current strategic plan and reassess the vision, mission and goals included at your next planning retreat. But try and set aside some time for education on a specific issue of development (e.g., planned giving, board committee development, etc.) This will allow your members to sink their teeth into one area of the plan and give them a better understanding of the work involved and where they can help.

✓ **Make sure the end product is an active plan.** In spite of best intentions, sometimes planning is the beginning and the end of the development process. Make sure your board knows that the plan will be put into action, in a timely manner with specific, measurable steps. Share specific examples of how the planning process has been successful in the past.

✓ **Engage persons with experience.** If you are fortunate enough to have someone on your board with prior fundraising experience, actively involve that person in spearheading the planning process. He/she will add credence to the importance of the retreat and the process, as well as professional insight. Just make sure they work with your facilitator in advance so they're not stepping on any toes.

Sources: Michael Alstad, Executive Director, Music Center of the Northwest, Seattle, WA. Phone (206) 526-8443. E-mail: malstd@mcnw.org
Dawn Welch, Asante Health System, Medford, OR. Phone (541) 472-7301. E-mail: Dwelch@asante.org

TURN TO BOARD MEMBERS, VOLUNTEERS AND GROUPS FOR HELP

Get Your Board to Assume Responsibility for Annual Gifts

It's not uncommon for boards to think it's the responsibility of staff to meet annual fund goals. That's wrong. Board members should feel some sense of ownership for meeting and exceeding annual gift goals.

Engage your board in annual giving by getting them to approve some portion of your annual giving goal. Depending on your board's size and level of past involvement, convince the board development committee to accept responsibility and seek full board approval for any of these yearly goals:

✓ To secure [X] number of gifts throughout the fiscal year within a defined gift range (i.e., $500 and above).

✓ To individually sell so many special event tickets each year (or purchase those they don't get sold).

✓ To individually contribute a minimum amount to the annual fund each year.

✓ To individually make a minimum number of solicitation calls on new prospects.

Turn Your Board Members Into Fundraisers

Want to get your board members more involved in fundraising? Just ask.

Staff with the nonprofit Advocates for Youth (Washington, DC) ask board members to fill out and sign a commitment form that outlines various ways they can help raise money for the organization throughout the year.

"It's important to recognize that some board members won't be comfortable fundraising, no matter what you do," says Elizabeth H. Merck, manager of individual giving. "The key is to figure out a way that they can get involved in fundraising that doesn't intimidate them."

The form provides about 20 options for board members to choose from, including:

❑ Serving on the fundraising committee.

❑ Making phone calls to thank donors for their gifts.

❑ Writing personal notes on fundraising appeal letters.

❑ Sending informational packets to five people by mail and asking them to make a gift.

❑ Providing the names of five individuals to add to the mailing list.

❑ Providing an introduction to at least one major donor prospect.

❑ Hosting an event.

❑ Pledging to search the Web using GoodSearch.

❑ Pledging to shop online using GiveBackAmerica.org.

Merck follows up with board members throughout the year to make sure they're fulfilling their commitments.

Source: Elizabeth H. Merck, Manager of Individual Giving, Advocates for Youth, Washington, DC. Phone (202) 419-3420 ext. 24. E-mail: liz@advocatesforyouth.org

Nurture Board Productivity

A common complaint among nonprofit workers is that their board isn't fully engaged in fundraising efforts. Likewise, board members complain about not being fully utilized.

So how do you bridge that gap and get your board on board?

Make specific requests of board members rather than just asking them to help in general, advises Dana Kindrick, executive administrative assistant, Navarro College Foundation (Corsicana, TX).

Tying board members to specific projects allows them to make their own best contribution. The following tips can help:

❑ **Know your board.** Every member should have a defined purpose prior to being asked to sit on a board. An attorney may help rewrite bylaws. A financial planner may help with planned gifts. Without defined roles, it's hard for board members to be effective.

❑ **Really know your board.** Fully vet your prospective board members. Don't be afraid to ask specifics about how many hours per month they can donate, what relationships they have that may be valuable to your cause and what roles they see

themselves taking. This will not scare off true prospects, and if it does, you're better off with that happening now than halfway through your capital campaign.

❑ **Make sure they know you.** Be clear about expectations before a prospective member accepts your offer. Have a set job description, guidelines for minimum board gifts and expected time commitment to help them make an informed decision.

❑ **Do an annual needs assessment for your board.** When you formally evaluate your board, you might be surprised to find you have four attorneys, but no financial planners. You might have a board full of people donating their own money, but are uncomfortable asking others to donate. An honest evaluation will help you right those situations for a more balanced and productive board.

Source: Dana Kindrick, Executive Administrative Assistant, Navarro College Foundation, Corsicana, TX. Phone (903) 875-7591. E-mail: dana.kindrick@navarrocollege.edu

TURN TO BOARD MEMBERS, VOLUNTEERS AND GROUPS FOR HELP

Focus on Enlisting, Grooming Volunteers

If you work for a nonprofit that consists of a one-person development shop, invest a portion of your time, as much as 50 percent, to enlist and nurture volunteers who can boost your fundraising efforts significantly.

Consider these recruitment and training efforts:

✓ **Set clear expectations for your board's development committee.** Prepare a committee job description. Meet regularly (outside of board meetings) with this group. Partner with them in identifying quantifiable objectives that they will be expected to meet throughout your fiscal year.

✓ **Start an auxiliary.** Pull together two or three individuals experienced at leading volunteers and get them to buy into what an auxiliary could accomplish for your nonprofit.

✓ **Form a special events committee.** Ask some experienced event planners to come up with one or more fundraisers for which they can take responsibility throughout the year — a golf classic, a fashion show or some other fundraiser that makes sense for your organization and the audience they intend to reach.

✓ **Hand pick a few dependable volunteers willing to assist with internal matters**: filing, data entry, mailings, phone reception and other duties that will free up your time to focus on more important matters.

✓ **Coordinate a community-wide volunteer-driven campaign.** Enlist co-chairs and captains who will then enlist others to conduct a highly visible 30-day campaign to raise funds from local businesses and individuals.

✓ **Form a planned gifts advisory board.** Assemble a small group representing agents of wealth — attorneys, trust officers, current planned gift donors, accountants — who will meet regularly to plan development, promotion and oversight of a planned gifts program on your behalf.

✓ **Establish a business partners program.** Call on a group of existing business donors to involve more businesses in the work of your organization. Come up with benefits for businesses that sponsor programs, make cash and in-kind donations and more.

Introductory Letter Helps Surface Possible Volunteers

Could you use more volunteers helping with fund development? You may find the help you seek through a simple invitation directed to names already on your mailing list.

While phone calls and particularly face-to-face visits are the most effective means of recruiting volunteers, a personalized letter with a bounce back might help to surface those who have any interest in assisting with some aspect of fund development.

Develop a simple letter (like the one shown here) to send to all or a portion of those on your mailing list. Once you have sent the letter and received responses back, follow up with phone calls and one-on-one meetings with those having expressed interest.

Volunteer Tip

- Don't assume that a no response from a possible volunteer means never. Timing may be a factor. Keep a list of those who reject your offer and re-approach them later.

Dear <Name>:

This time I am not writing to ask for your financial support but rather your time.

To better meet the needs of those we serve, we need to generate far more financial resources than we have in the past. And to do that, we need the volunteer assistance of individuals who care about what we do and what we hope to accomplish.

Could you give one hour of your time? Would you be willing to serve on a committee or sign letters? What about joining me in making calls on those who have given in the past — to thank them for their generosity?

Whatever you can do, whatever you feel comfortable in doing, will be gratefully appreciated.

If we are to expand our programs and accelerate what we are able to accomplish, we need the volunteer help of people such as you.

Please review the enclosed checklist of ways in which you can assist with our fund development efforts, then check those that interest you and return the form. Once we receive it, we will be in touch with you to answer questions and discuss next steps.

Thank you in advance for giving positive consideration to this important request.

Sincerely,

Plug Volunteers Into Annual Planning Efforts

Would you like volunteers to become more engaged in your fundraising efforts? Then involve them in planning your year and in shaping specific fundraising strategies.

Whether it is by participating a planning retreat, being a part of a focus group or meeting with you individually, ask for volunteer input that will set the stage for continued involvement as the fundraising year progresses.

Volunteers can help plan by:

- Reviewing and commenting on your yearly plan.
- Brainstorming new approaches for increasing overall gifts.
- Planning a yearly campaign kickoff event.
- Reviewing and commenting on specific fundraising programs (i.e., phonathon, community campaign, gift clubs and accompanying benefits, etc.)
- Brainstorming funding opportunities that appeal to the giving public.

TURN TO BOARD MEMBERS, VOLUNTEERS AND GROUPS FOR HELP

Tips for Training Volunteer Solicitors

Building a group of proficient volunteer solicitors doesn't happen over night.

- **Begin by identifying and enlisting those who are existing ambassadors.** Who among your board, key volunteers and donors are already selling your organization in their everyday lives? These individuals are prime solicitor candidates because they are already committed to your cause.

- **Train those who will eventually train others.** Once you have identified the handful of volunteers already committed, ask for their two-year involvement as you build a volunteer solicitation program. In year one, they will be expected to help you solicit gifts from a list of agreed-to prospects. In year two, they will help to recruit and train additional volunteers.

- **Be prepared to give them the attention they deserve.** Knowing that your solicitation efforts will eventually multiply, meet at least monthly as a group and also make some joint calls with each volunteer to improve their solicitation proficiency and confidence.

- **Make the most of your meeting time.** Use group meetings to review lists of nondonors who you hope to convert to contributors, lists of existing donors who volunteers may help to upgrade, and ask volunteers for names of prospects who are on neither of your lists.

- **Keep spoon-feeding information that will help them become effective sales persons.** The more familiar these volunteers become with your organization's accomplishments, the more effectively they can sell your institution to others.

  This investment of time will help to multiply your solicitation effectiveness.

Report Form Helps Solicitors Fulfill Expectations

When enlisting board members and volunteers in gift solicitation, be sure to provide them with an easy-to-understand form they can use to fulfill what's expected of them.

Although you will no doubt send marketing materials, pledge forms and perhaps additional information with them on prospect calls, note that a prospect profile and solicitation report such as the template shown here will provide key information about the prospect and help volunteer solicitors stay on track throughout the solicitation process.

PROSPECT PROFILE AND SOLICITATION REPORT
— FOR INDIVIDUALS —

Lead Solicitor _____
Secondary Solicitors_____
Prospect _____
Home Address_____
City _____ State _____ ZIP _____
Home Phone _____ E-mail_____
Business _____ Title_____
Business Address _____
Business Phone _____ E-mail_____
Spouse _____
Relationship to [Name of Charity] _____

5-YEAR HISTORY OF CONTRIBUTIONS TO [NAME OF CHARITY]

YEAR	AMOUNT	PURPOSE
2006	$5,000	Unrestricted (Annual Fund)
2007	$7,000	Unrestricted (Annual Fund)
2008	$7,000	Unrestricted (Annual Fund)
2009	$7,500	Unrestricted (Annual Fund)

Amount to be Solicited $ _____

SOLICITATION RESULTS

Date of Solicitation _____
☐ **Yes**   Amount $_____   Form of Gift _____
      If pledged, over what period of time? _____
      Beginning _____ Ending _____
      Use of gift _____
☐ **No**   Reason: _____
☐ **Decision Pending**   Planned Follow-up: _____
_____

Additional Comments Regarding Prospect: _____
_____
_____

Please use back of form to record key discussion points of call. Return to [Name of Organization]

TURN TO BOARD MEMBERS, VOLUNTEERS AND GROUPS FOR HELP

Committees Should Have Yearly Goals and Objectives

Just as paid staff should have yearly goals and objectives — as identified in an operational plan — volunteers involved with fund development should also have a yearlong plan of action. Whether it's a major gifts committee, a development committee, a special events committee or some other ongoing group, work with a committee's members to identify quantifiable objectives supporting internal goals and objectives. And rather than informing them of their responsibilities, engage them in a planning process that helps them more fully own those objectives.

Once goals and objectives have been established for a committee, the written document should be monitored at regular meetings to measure progress being made throughout the year. Having such a plan of action for your committee will help to keep them focused on achieving what matters most throughout the year.

Develop a yearly plan of action for each of your committees involved with various aspects of fund development. Here's a plan that illustrates one committee's yearly objectives.

Content not available in this edition

An Annual Fund Committee Might Be the Ticket For You

Providing you're willing to give it the attention it deserves, an active annual fund committee or membership committee can make a big difference in expanding your donor base and moving donors to higher levels of giving.

Select willing, enthusiastic volunteers from among existing donors as you recruit committee members. Ask them to serve at least a two-year term so you can stagger those coming on and going off the committee from year to year.

Here are 10 examples of what your committee can do to reach new levels of annual giving support:

1. Regularly review lists of nondonors with the purpose of selecting names for face-to-face calls.

2. Conduct a telesolicitation effort in which they recruit additional volunteers to phone prospects over a three- or four-day period.

3. Host individual receptions in their homes (or elsewhere) to introduce your organization to new prospects.

4. Conduct a thank-a-thon with face-to-face and/or phone calls to donors who gave above a certain level during the previous fiscal year.

5. Refer names of and make calls on friends, associates and relatives.

6. Organize a new special event attracting new supporters and providing valuable visibility for your cause.

7. Organize a personalized letter-writing campaign in which volunteers write letters to people they know, inviting them to make a first-time gift.

8. Conduct a fourth-quarter effort to contact persons with unpaid pledges, encouraging them to contribute before year-end.

9. Host a kickoff reception at the beginning of your fiscal year complete with a catchy theme and lots of enthusiasm.

10. Coordinate a year-end celebration that thanks annual fund donors and keeps the annual fund visible in the eyes of donors and the public.

TURN TO BOARD MEMBERS, VOLUNTEERS AND GROUPS FOR HELP

Help Current Contributors Attract New Ones

Make it easy and inviting for your current contributors to invite their circle of friends, family and associates to support your cause as well. Just imagine how your numbers of annual contributors would mushroom if you could convince even 10 percent of your current donors to obtain a gift from someone. What would that amount to in new contributors for your institution or agency?

To encourage current contributors to help with fund development, draft a letter they can use as a guide in crafting a message of their own. Then send the draft letter to all current contributors along with your request and instructions on how they can go about inviting others to give. (See the examples below.)

Plea and letter of instruction to current contributors.

Sample letter current contributors can use to draft their own appeal.

Dear [Name of Prospect]:

I'm writing to only a handful of people like you who I consider special — special because I feel you'll understand where I'm coming from when I ask you for some help.

As you may or may not know, I have been contributing to XYZ Center for a number of years now. They are doing such wonderful things there, and I can think of no more deserving cause to support.

But they could do so much more if the resources were available. And that's why I'm writing to you. I'd really appreciate it if you'd consider making a contribution to the Center. They could use it and I wouldn't be urging you to do this if I didn't think you'd find it to be a rewarding experience.

[Name], whatever you choose to do, thanks for giving it your consideration.

Your friend,

[Name]

P.S. If by chance you are a current contributor to XYZ Center, thank you! I'm proud that you are a fellow supporter of this deserving cause.

Dear [Name of Current Contributor]:

We are so very grateful for the contributions you make to our center each year. You know by your actions that support is needed and makes a noticeable difference in what we are able to achieve.

That's why I am asking you to help us in another way. Please contact any of your friends, family and/or associates who you think might be willing to make a gift to the Center. If each of our current contributors could convince even one person or business to make a gift, we would double the number of those currently giving to XYZ Center. And what a shot in the arm that would provide in allowing us to do even more!

I've enclosed a sample letter you can use as a guide in drafting a letter of your own. But remember, the letter should be written in your own words since it's coming from you. I've also enclosed five return envelopes you can enclose in each letter you send out. (If you need more return envelopes, I'll have them to you in a jiffy!)

Could you please identify who you want to write to and have your letters prepared (on your own stationary) and sent within two weeks? Once you have sent your letters, simply complete and return the enclosed prospect list to us so we can track your results. We'll keep you informed of those who make a gift based on your letter.

[Name], thank you in advance for your leadership in contacting others on our behalf! We're counting on you and others to help make this a truly successful effort.

Most sincerely,

[Your Name]

Form a Volunteer-driven Sponsorship Committee

Use this sample description as a tool to set up your own sponsorship committee.

To increase revenue from sponsorships, why not establish a sponsorship committee whose members meet periodically and enlist new sponsors for current and new projects?

Having a sponsorship committee accomplishes several positive goals. For example:

1. It allows you to make more sponsorship contacts than you could ever hope to do on your own.

2. It increases your odds for success since committee members may have greater leverage in securing some sponsorships.

3. The committee can help return current sponsors by having them serve on the committee.

4. It offers another volunteer involvement opportunity in fund development efforts.

SPONSORSHIP COMMITTEE MEMBERSHIP AND RESPONSIBILITIES

The primary purpose of the Sponsorship Committee is to help generate additional revenue for [Name of Organization] through new and renewed sponsorships. The Committee is also charged with evaluating all aspects of the sponsorship program and making recommendations to the Development Office.

Committee Membership

The Sponsorship Committee shall include no less than six individuals, at least three of whom shall represent current or past sponsors. Committee members shall serve a term of at least two years.

Committee Responsibilities

1. Sponsorship Committee members will meet no less than quarterly.

2. Committee members will meet to:
   A. Review existing names of potential sponsors and identify new prospects.
   B. Determine which committee members will contact particular sponsor prospects.
   C. Work with current sponsors to ensure compliance with sponsorship agreements.
   D. Work with Development Office personnel to identify new sponsorship opportunities at [Name of Organization].
   E. Determine stewardship actions to be taken with current sponsors.
   F. Review procedures and policies related to sponsorships and make recommendations.

TURN TO BOARD MEMBERS, VOLUNTEERS AND GROUPS FOR HELP

Target Particular Groups With Involvement Opportunities

Want to generate more and increased gifts? Work at increasing involvement among both donors and would-be donors. As you know, involvement leads to investment.

To improve the level of involvement, however, strive to offer opportunities matching the interests of particular groups. For example, the volunteer projects you suggest to former board members may be different than those you would offer young professionals or recent high school graduates.

Examples of segmentation may include:

- Alumni
- Specific professions
- Singles
- Young families
- Retired employees
- Women/men
- New graduates
- Scout or 4-H groups
- Baby boomers
- Parents
- Businesses
- Civic organizations
- Senior citizens
- Former board members
- Environmental activists
- Church groups
- Community service opportunities
- Families of those you serve

After identifying targeted groups, develop involvement opportunity menus aimed at their interests and/or skills. Then market those opportunities through one-on-one visits, direct mail, online, group presentations and more.

This is an example of an inquiry card that could be used to encourage former board members to renew their involvement with a nonprofit.

Elkhorn Council
on Sexual Assault & Domestic Violence

Involvement Opportunities for Former Board Members...

Name _____
Address_____
City/State/ZIP _____
Phone _____ E-mail_____

- ❑ Mentor a new board member
- ❑ Host a reception
- ❑ Conduct stewardship calls
- ❑ Screen prospect names
- ❑ Make business contacts
- ❑ Help identify awards recipients
- ❑ Help host appreciation banquet
- ❑ Conduct VIP tours
- ❑ Help make new introductions
- ❑ Other_____

Show Clubs, Civic Groups How They Can Help

Do you give presentations to area clubs and civic organizations? Although education and awareness are no doubt a big part of those engagements, be sure to show those groups what they can do to help your cause.

Here's a sampling of what you can do:

- Share a printed wish list of needs from which clubs can select and help to address.

- Invite them to coordinate their own fundraising event with proceeds going to your charity.

- Distribute brochures that encourage individual members to contribute to your cause.

- Ask clubs to sponsor or adopt a particular program as volunteers — one that fits their mission.

- Partner with a group to sell something and split proceeds: ornaments, calendars, cookbooks, etc.

- Invite the club's members to help staff one of your daylong events.

Train Chapters to Raise Funds on Your Behalf

The saying goes: "Give a man a fish and you feed him for a day; teach a man to fish and you feed him for a lifetime."

That same principal applies to teaching chapter members to raise funds in their communities on your behalf: If you invest the time to train them, you will have invested in the overall success of the chapter itself, as well as benefits the chapter can bring to your organization.

Helping chapter members raise funds in their own communities on your behalf (rather than you attempting to do so long-distance) just makes sense. They know the territory and, if willing and properly trained, are in a far better position to raise funds than someone not from the area.

To train chapter leaders to raise funds for your organization:

1. Provide templates for direct mail appeals that they can tailor to their particular needs. With templates in hand, they can produce letters, sign them, stuff and mail the appeals.

2. Train one or two people willing to organize a volunteer-driven phonathon. Those chairs can then recruit and train volunteers willing to make phone calls. Provide them with templates of scripts, caller cards, step-by-step procedures and more.

3. Invite chapter leaders to organize special events in their communities. Give them examples of fundraisers from which they can choose.

4. Conduct a training session for each chapter on procedures and techniques for making personal calls on individuals and businesses. Organize teams; include time for practice solicitation. Provide handouts of brochures, pledge forms and such they can take with them.

WORK TO IMPROVE DIRECT MAIL APPEAL RESULTS

As costly and ineffective as the postal system has become in recent years, direct mail continues to offer one viable means of generating annual gift revenue. It's just more important that you give careful thought to the makeup of your audience, the message, the timing and frequency of your appeals and the appeal package. Analyze past appeals' success. Test new approaches to targeted audience. Recognize that "one size fits all" doesn't work anymore.

Analyze Appeal to Improve Future Results

Which of your direct mail appeals was most productive last year? Which resulted in the greatest dollar return? What was the average gift size from each mailing? How much did it cost to raise each dollar?

It makes good sense to monitor and analyze your direct mail costs and results throughout the course of each year and prior to drafting an operational plan for the upcoming year. Doing so will provide a quantitative measure of what works and what doesn't work.

Complete a direct mail cost analysis report (example shown to the right) to track costs and results of solicitation appeals throughout the year.

Content not available in this edition

Map Out Yearly Direct Mail Appeals

To maximize gift revenue returns from direct mail, plan a year's worth of appeals in advance.

Using historical data, schedule a year's worth of appeals aimed at particular segments of your database (past contributors, non-donors, affinity groups, etc.), inviting support for particular funding projects.

There may be instances when an appeal is directed to your entire mailing list and others restricted to one or more segments of your database. Funding projects may vary from appeal to appeal as well.

2009 APPEALS SCHEDULE

Date	Audience	Size	Project	Comments
1/15	Past Contributors	2,234	Operations	
3/1	Past Contributors	2,234	Operations	Follow up: Non-responders
4/15	Area Businesses	3,040	Sponsorships	Multiple choices
6/12	Non-donors	6,466	Three projects	Multiple choices
9/15	Planned Gift Prospects	883	Planned gift invite	Includes bounce back
11/15	Lybunt Appeal	2,234	Operations	Follow up: Non-responders
12/1	Entire Database	8,700	Holiday Wish List	Multiple choices

Having a yearly schedule of appeals, such as the example shown here, helps to visualize the big picture and spot potential problems or missed opportunities. You may even choose to include other types of mailings (e.g., newsletters, invitations, announcements) in your schedule.

Appeal Writing Tip

- While an appeal letter may convey a sense of urgency, don't overdo it to the point of sounding desperate. Although people like to know their gifts are making a noticeable difference, they also want to believe the cause they are supporting will be in existence a year from now.

Direct Mail Tips

- **Measure cost versus net.** When evaluating the cost of a given appeal package, recognize that the more expensive the appeal may yield the greatest net income.

- **Don't limit yourself to one ask per year.** Most donors give based on how much they can afford to give at any one time, not how much they give during the course of the year.

WORK TO IMPROVE DIRECT MAIL APPEAL RESULTS

Keep Refining Your Yearlong Direct Mail Appeal Plan

It's wise to have a 12-month written plan that outlines all direct mail appeals you'll be sending to particular groups throughout the upcoming year. It makes even more sense to refine that plan as you move from one year to another.

Create a calendar that identifies all planned appeals for the year, including those directed to past contributors and non-donors. Then, as you near the completion of the current year, formulate a new calendar for the subsequent year that includes revisions to the previous year's schedule.

This year-to-year comparison of direct mail appeals helps identify which segments of your database will be receiving particular invitations to support your organization.

The example shown here includes personalized anniversary letters to those who gave during a particular month in the prior year.

Sunset Retirement Community: Yearlong Appeals Plan		
Drop Date	2008 Appeals	2009 Appeals
1/3	Anniversary Letter January '08 contributors	Anniversary Letter January '09 contributors
1/15	Non-donor Businesses (50-mile radius)	Non-donor Businesses (50-mile radius)
2/3	Anniversary Letter February '08 contributors	Anniversary Letter February '09 contributors
2/15		Special Memorial Appeal: Families of former residents
3/3	Anniversary Letter March '08 contributors	Anniversary Letter March '09 contributors
4/3	Anniversary Letter April '08 contributors	Anniversary Letter April '09 contributors
4/15	Non-donor local residents	Non-donor local residents
5/3	Anniversary Letter May '08 Contributors	Anniversary Letter May '09 Contributors
6/3	Anniversary Letter June '08 contributors	Anniversary Letter June '09 contributors
7/3	Anniversary Letter July '08 contributors	Anniversary Letter July '09 contributors
8/3	Anniversary Letter August '08 contributors	Anniversary Letter August '09 contributors
9/3	Anniversary Letter September '08 contributors	Anniversary Letter September '09 contributors
9/15		Special appeal: $250 prospects
10/3	Anniversary Letter October '08 contributors	Anniversary Letter October '09 contributors
11/3	Anniversary Letter November '08 contributors	Anniversary Letter November '09 contributors
11/10	General Appeal (entire list excluding current contributors)	General Appeal (entire list excluding current contributors)
12/3	Anniversary Letter November '08 contributors	Anniversary Letter November '09 contributors

An Appeal Letter's First Paragraph Is Key

When the recipient of a direct mail appeal receives your letter, there's no telling how much of it he/she will read. Some people go immediately to the P.S. while others may read only the first paragraph and stop there. That's why that first paragraph needs to grab the reader's attention and call the reader to action.

When you begin to draft an appeal, start by writing three or four different introductory paragraphs. Assume that paragraph will be the only message the recipient reads. Knowing that, what message do you really want to convey to the reader? What can you say that will motivate him/her to make a contribution?

After completing a few introductory paragraphs, set them aside and then re-read them later in the day with a fresh set of eyes. Which paragraph most gets your message across? Which packs the most punch? Which is the most explicit call to action?

Once you have that first paragraph solidified, the paragraphs that follow can provide additional backup information that furthers your case.

Consider an Attention-grabbing, Stand-alone Statement

Your appeal letter should accomplish three things: 1) grab the attention of the recipient, 2) provide a compelling message and 3) move the recipient to action.

Part of the attention-grabbing element can include an opening statement or question that attracts the reader's focus and makes him/her want to learn more.

These stand-alone messages could include facts that justify your reason for asking for support: "One in eight women in our county has been abused in the past year." Or, the aim of your message may be to evoke emotion: "Eight-year-old Abby won't get the nutrition her body needs unless people like you care enough to step forward."

Whatever approach you take, use the stand-alone statement to grab readers' attention and begin making your case for a gift.

Hopkins Foodbank, Inc.

September 2005

Mr. & Mrs. Alden Lane
8 Richards Drive
Hopkins, AL

Dear Mr. and Mrs. Lane:

"Can you imagine what it would be like not knowing if you would be able to put food on the table for your children?"

That's the fear that a surprising number of families in our area face each day....

WORK TO IMPROVE DIRECT MAIL APPEAL RESULTS

Nine Ways to Improve Direct Mail Appeals

With all of the competition for philanthropic dollars, appeal letters not only need to grab the attention of would-be donors, they need to be as compelling as possible, too.

By putting some thought into your letter and appeal package and paying attention to key details, you can increase both the number and size of gifts received from your mailings.

Here are nine solid ways to help give your 2009 appeal letters more of what it takes to move readers to make gifts:

1. Keep letters brief, neatly spaced, error-free and grammatically correct.

2. Verify spelling of all names and proper titles of each individual.

3. Avoid use of words you wouldn't use in normal, everyday conversations. You don't want to look as if you studied your thesaurus just to impress them, and you don't want your readers to have to get out the dictionary to understand your message.

4. Use emotional adjectives sparingly. Almost every appeal leans heavily on "urgent" needs and "critical" situations. Convey your message with less used but still familiar, moving words.

5. Watch punctuation and style. Too many italicized, boldfaced or underlined passages clutter your page and detract from the message. Use exclamation marks only in proper context, not as an attention-getting gimmick.

6. Remember: Writing a short letter takes more effort than writing a long one. Ask an objective staff member to help with the editing process to make your piece as concise as possible while still having the impact you desire.

7. Don't send your first draft. Read your letter two or three times, or until all superfluous wording is eliminated.

8. Sign your name in real ink. Time taken to sign in a contrasting ink color shows you take a personal interest.

9. Be descriptive and direct. Writing "volunteers spent more than 100 hours each weekend collecting canned goods" tells your story much better than cliches such as: "We are striving to set new standards of excellence in the services we offer to those in need."

Boost Your Appeal Response Rate

Standard operating procedure: Send a mass appeal and hope people will give.

Kick up your response rate: The number of recipients to earmark for a phone call depends on the number of people available to make the calls. Count on one person being responsible for 10 to 20 calls and use staff or volunteers to figure out a practical number of phone call attempts that can be completed within two weeks of the mailing.

Write a Simple, Concise Call to Action; Repeat

An effective fundraising appeal includes a simple and specific call to action that answers the reader's question: "Now that I care, how can I help?"

"A call to action is how the recipient can make a difference and create an impact," says Theresa Nelson, founder and principal, Theresa Nelson and Associates (Oakland, CA). "It's the place and time when you ask the recipient of the message to do something — make a donation, sign a petition, call an elected official or volunteer after a disaster."

One mistake development professionals make when writing a call to action? Overcomplicating it, says Nelson, which detracts from the message and dilutes its impact.

To write an effective call to action, Nelson says:

- Be clear and concise about what this one person can do now to make a difference.

- Use active verbs that create momentum in your message.

- Quantify the impact of the action, equating the reader's act to some specific change.

- Ask yourself, "How can I ...?" Make sure your message clearly answers that question.

Additionally, repeat the message throughout your direct mail pieces, she says. "It should be in the letter at least twice, early within the first few paragraphs and usually in the postscript. It may also be on the outer envelope to preview the letter. In an e-mail, the upper-right hand portion of the body of the e-mail is considered the best position for a call-to-action box, with the message repeated in the text and often in a graphic caption."

Why so much repetition? "You need to circle back to the reason you are communicating," says Nelson. "You give the reader a reason for continuing to read, because just reading about a problem without illuminating the solution can be depressing. You need to provide for readers the answer to the question, 'Now that I care, how can I ...' at least once in the letter or e-mail text, as well as graphically."

Source: Theresa Nelson, Founder and Principal, Theresa Nelson and Associates, Oakland, CA. Phone (510) 420-0539. E-mail: theresa@theresanelson.com

Effective Call-to-action Messages

Theresa Nelson, founder and principal, Theresa Nelson and Associates (Oakland, CA), shares two on-the-mark calls to action and explains why they work:

Example 1: After a recent address by President Obama on the economy, the website http://my.barackobama.com/page/content/budgetaction and coordinated e-mails said, "Watch President Obama's message and get involved in the effort to make this plan a reality by calling your elected representatives and by joining a canvass this weekend.'
Call to action: Watch the message and join a canvass this weekend.

Example 2: Doctors Without Borders seeks aid workers with the message, "Put your ideals into practice. All prospective medical and nonmedical aid workers: Join us for a presentation, film and question-and-answer session to learn more about how you can become part of Doctors Without Borders' field work. A recruiter will be on hand to discuss requirements and the application process. "
Call to action: Put your ideals into practice; join Doctors Without Borders in the field.

WORK TO IMPROVE DIRECT MAIL APPEAL RESULTS

Use Response Cards With Direct Mail, Face-to-face Calls

Every face-to-face or direct mail contact you have with people should allow you to invite their involvement with your organization in some capacity. Whether meeting with a first-time or long-time donor, the individual's growing involvement with your institution is the single most important factor in generating new or increased gifts, needed volunteer assistance, or both.

So what systems do you have in place that help to show you when someone may be interested? How do you know when someone might want to establish a scholarship? How do you know someone wants to get involved in planning a special event? When someone is willing to assist in your capital campaign?

The use of response cards or bounce backs should be incorporated whenever and wherever possible. Whenever a new brochure is developed, include an accompanying response card. Whenever correspondence is sent, include a response card. Whenever you meet with anyone, select a response card that best fits the circumstances and share it with the prospect.

The response card gives others a tangible reason to get back to you. And when they do, you don't have to guess or read minds. You have evidence that they have expressed interest in learning more about your organization and perhaps, how they can assist your efforts.

As you can see from the examples here, there is no limit on the number of ways in which you can use this simple tool. Assess the many ways in which bounce backs may be useful in your work.

Examples of bounce backs that can accompany various types of brochures and mailings.

> Pleased to meet you.... Let's get to know each other.
>
> Name _____
> Address _____
> City _____ State _____ ZIP _____
> Daytime Phone _____
> Evening Phone _____
> Occupation _____ Title _____
>
> I'm interested in learning more about the following:
>
> ☐ The college's history and mission.
> ☐ Distinguishing achievements of the college.
> ☐ Course offerings/majors.
> ☐ Career advising.
> ☐ Financial aid/scholarship assistance.
> ☐ Upcoming calendar of events.
> ☐ Speakers bureau topics.
> ☐ Volunteer opportunities.
> ☐ Exploring planned gift opportunities.
> ☐ Annual fund opportunities.
> ☐ Endowed gift opportunities.
> ☐ How to establish a scholarship.
> ☐ The college's future plans.
> ☐ Alumni activities and involvement.
> ☐ Distinguished graduates of the institution.
> ☐ Status of the endowment.
> ☐ Other _____

> ...rn More About How to Establish a Scholarship
>
> ...me _____
> ...dress _____
> ...y _____ State _____ ZIP _____
> ...ytime Phone _____
> ...ning Phone _____
> ...cupation _____ Title _____
>
> ...ould like to learn more about establishing or
> ...ding to a named scholarship. Please provide me
> ...h additional information on the following topic(s):
>
> ...How scholarships help students.
> ...How scholarships help the college.
> ...How scholarships help our society.
> ...How to establish a named scholarship.
> ...Using memorial gifts to establish a scholarship.
> ...Annual scholarships and how they work.
> ...Endowed scholarships and how they work.
> ...Placing restrictions on scholarships.
> ...Establishing or adding to a scholarship through
> ...my estate.
> ...Selection of scholarship recipients.
> ...Meeting the recipients of my scholarship.
> ...Potential tax benefits of establishing a
> ...olarship.

Pay Attention to the Appeal Package

When sending a direct mail appeal, recognize that your letter is not the only thing that impacts the response rate. The ancillary items that accompany your letter play an influential role as well. Consider these six points with regard to each direct mail package:

1. Develop a reply or pledge card that stands on its own. Readers will more likely misplace or toss your letter than they will the reply card.

2. Consider using a eye-catching teaser phrase on your envelope, but remember: A poorly written teaser or one in poor taste is worse than no teaser at all.

3. If you're mailing standard rate, consider using stamps as opposed to a meter tape or mailing indicia. Hand-affixed stamps reduce the chance of the piece getting tossed because it looks like junk mail.

4. If you're mailing first class, consider using a commemorative stamp that has meaning for your organization.

5. Before your package is printed, have more than one individual proof each piece. Doublecheck all e-mail and Web addresses, phone numbers and all contact information. Spot typos or stiff phrasing by reading articles backward, starting with the last paragraph and working up to the first.

Appeal Letter Ideas

- If you're approaching someone with celebrity status to sign an appeal letter (i.e., board member, community leader, corporate CEO), why not take it a step further? Get his/her commitment to personally thank the 25 largest contributors who respond to the letter.

Direct Mail Appeal Tips

- Send an e-mail follow-up message to those who have not responded to a recent direct mail appeal. Be sure to offer the option of making an online gift.

- If your goal is to build your donor base, ask non-donors for small gifts directed to particular projects form which they can choose. Once that first gift is made, you can focus on building a habit of giving

WORK TO IMPROVE DIRECT MAIL APPEAL RESULTS

Make Sure Smaller Donors Know Their Donations Matter

Jamie Leszczynski, associate director of annual giving, The Fund for Oswego (Oswego, NY) is hoping to strike gold with the department's most recent direct mail appeal to benefit the State University at New York (SUNY) Oswego.

The mailing, sent in February 2009 to 7,774 of Graduates of the Last Decade (GOLD), is intended to show how even the small donations are important and add up.

Leszczynski says the idea came from the fundraising committee of a leadership council created specifically to target this group of alumni. The committee reviewed marketing pieces from the last several years and compiled suggestions and recommendations.

The committee wanted something short and simple, all in one piece, she says. Planners chose $25 as the target donation to keep it affordable for everyone.

The marketing piece, shown to the right, shows donors: "If every graduate from Oswego in the past 10 years gave a gift of $25 this year, the college could support students with an additional $380,925."

Leszczynski says feedback for the piece has been positive, with 42 percent of gifts to date coming from first-time donors. Thirty-eight percent of the donors responding to the piece gave more than the suggested $25, including three who gave $100 each.

She notes that the project has reaped a valuable lesson for the fund's staff: "Get alumni involved with reviewing your pieces and have them assist with the text. They know what they want to see and what works for them."

Source: Jamie Stack Leszczynski, Associate Director of Annual Giving, The Fund for Oswego, SUNY Oswego, Oswego, NY. Phone (315) 312-3121. E-mail: leszczyn@oswego.edu

Direct mail pieces from a campaign for The Fund for Oswego, SUNY Oswego (Oswego, NY) target graduates from the last decade with an ask of just $25, emphasizing "every gift counts."

Content not available in this edition

Content not available in this edition

Content not available in this edition

Content not available in this edition

Try Testing Back-to-back Appeals

Think of all the junk mail you receive at home. Much of it hardly gets a glance before it's off to the trash. And sometimes mail you may have read in other circumstances — more time on your hands, less stressed, etc. — gets lumped in with the junk mail.

That's the same way many of those to whom you send an appeal might react. Under some circumstances your letter will get pitched without even having been opened, while in others, the recipient might read it and positively respond with a gift. That's why you should periodically test back-to-back mailings to the same group.

Send an appeal to a smaller segment of your mailing list. Then, say 30 or 45 days later, send another appeal to those in the same group who didn't respond to the first mailing. Begin the second letter with a messages such as: "Just in case you missed our first invitation to support an important and deserving project...."

Measure the response of both mailings. Evaluate items such as percentage that responded with a gift to each mailing; average gift size; number of responses; amount generated from each mailing; cost/revenue ratio; etc. Then weigh those stats against any negative responses you received from those who received two mailings in a row.

By testing back-to-back appeals with smaller groups, you can determine whether to use that method for a larger scale campaign.

Follow-up Appeal Messages

Use follow-up messages on both your outer envelope and your letter's opening statement....

✓ We missed hearing back from you.

✓ Your absence was noticed.

✓ It won't be the same without your participation.

✓ Just in case you overlooked our first invitation....

WORK TO IMPROVE DIRECT MAIL APPEAL RESULTS

Add Personalized Brochure in Your Annual Fund Mailings

The more personal you can make a mailing, the better the chance the recipient will open it, read it and lend support to your cause.

Bridget Snow, principal and creative director, Bridget Snow Design (Warwick, RI), says an alternative to a traditional personalized letter and mass-produced brochure is a personalized brochure using variable data printing — a form of on-demand printing that lets you change text, graphics and images within individual pieces in a single database or external file in the same print run.

"Tastefully crafting a tailored personalized brochure can grab an individual reader's interest, and is in some cases more effective than the standard personalized letter, which has saturated the marketplace," says Snow. Variables can include message changes according to giving level; photos/graphics and specific messages and visuals specific to academic/extracurricular activities.

Snow says two factors determine cost-effectiveness of variable data printing: total press run and number of customized elements.

These examples show how quantity and number of customizations impact cost:

Project: Four-color self-mailer for independent school's annual fund campaign.
Total run: 5,000 pieces in lots of 3,500 and 1,500, each requiring variable imagery.
Option A: Traditionally printed four-color process on two sides; variable black plate on both sides.
Option B: Traditionally printed four-color process on one side; variable black on both sides and variable four-color on one side.
Snow says the Option B quote came in higher by 40 percent.

Project: Reunion invitation
Total run: 800 pieces, comprising 11 sets of variables in four-color self-mailer.

Option A: Traditional four-color process and a variable black plate.
Option B: All variable four-color process.

Snow says that because quantity was a significant production factor, using totally variable printing the job (Option B) cost 21 percent less than Option A.

Source: Bridget Snow, Principal/Creative Director, Bridget Snow Design, Warwick, RI. Phone (401) 781-2224. E-mail: bsnow@bsnowdesign.com. Website: www.bsnowdesign.com

Content not available in this edition

This mailer shows how certain aspects can be personalized, from recipient to photos to specific messages.

Try These Proven Direct Mail Techniques

Although some organizations are shying away from direct mail, a well-orchestrated campaign is still an effective and profitable method of raising funds.

Mary Richardson, director of strategic planning, Huntsinger & Jeffer (Richmond, VA), shares four current techniques proven to increase direct mail response rates.

1. **Avoid the standard No. 10 window envelope.** "The United States Postal Service has been restructuring postage rates to make non-standard formats more expensive to mail," Richardson says. "But they are still worth testing to determine if the additional cost might produce an even larger jump in response." She suggests three alternatives:

   - Smaller, squarer envelopes that either are, or appear to be, personally addressed;
   - Larger envelopes that imply importance; or
   - Lumpy or three-dimensional formats to grab attention.

2. **Send mailings to high-value donors first class, not bulk mail.** Richardson says this not only ensures a higher rate of delivery, but also suggests a sense of importance.

3. **Offer specific and tangible ways to support your appeal.** For instance, she suggests explaining that a donation of $x will provide books and supplies for a student. "Everyone involved in philanthropy wants to be part of something bigger than themselves," Richardson says. "The most successful fundraising allows donors to take ownership of the specific part they've chosen for themselves."

> ### Direct Mail Tip
> - Include a deadline when asking for a gift. "Your response by Oct. 1 will help ensure our project gets realized."

4. **Develop and maintain a good reputation.** "Remember, direct mail does not exist in a vacuum," Richardson says. "The visibility and reputation that an organization maintains in the outside world has a stronger impact on response rates than any direct mail tactic or technique."

Source: Mary Richardson, Director of Strategic Planning, Huntsinger & Jeffer, Richmond, VA. Phone (804) 266-2499. E-mail: maryrich1@comcast.net

WORK TO IMPROVE DIRECT MAIL APPEAL RESULTS

Personalized Message Makes for Direct Mail Appeal Success

An appeal with a simple tagline, "Then, Now and Again," has yielded the best results in direct mail campaign history for the Hebrew Academy of Tidewater/Strelitz Early Childhood Center (Virginia Beach, VA).

Eilene Rosenblum, director of development, says each piece of the direct mail appeal is a four-fold, 5 1/2 X 9-inch brochure featuring a school year photo of a donor juxtaposed with a present family photo (where the children are the current students).

A quote from the donor expressing gratitude for life lessons learned at the academy is featured under the family photo, with information on his/her subsequent education.

The brochure's next two pages feature text on the school's mission and need for financial support, mixed with photos of students who attend the K-6 and preschool division.

Mailed in three parts — August, December and April — the direct mail appeal was sent to 3,000 donors and prospective donors.

Unlike past years when donors who contributed after the first mailing were not sent additional mailings, Rosenblum says all 3,000 persons on the list received all three mailings, plus a thank-you note if they donated, so they could see the complete campaign.

This tactic — along with the use of former students at the center of the appeal's message — proved a winning combination, bringing in 500 gifts totaling more than $350,000. The average gift was $500 and the largest, $2,500.

"This approach yielded the best results for a direct mail appeal we have ever produced," says Rosenblum, pointing to the $50,000 increase in gifts over the prior year's annual campaign.

> "The personalized appeal resonated with recipients not only because they recognized themselves, but because they recognized their contemporaries."

"The personalized appeal resonated with recipients not only because they recognized themselves, but because they recognized their contemporaries. It also resonated with older people who saw their children or their children's children following in their footsteps."

Rosenblum says the mailing was such a success she is using it again next year, featuring new participants and their families.

Source: Eilene Rosenblum, Director of Development, Hebrew Academy of Tidewater/Strelitz Early Childhood Center, Virginia Beach, VA. Phone (757) 424-4327. E-mail: Ehrosenblum@hebrewacademy.net

Content not available in this edition

Juxtaposing a past class picture with the student today proved successful for a direct mail appeal for the Hebrew Academy of Tidewater/Strelitz Early Childhood Center (Virginia Beach, VA).

Add Postscript to Direct Mail Appeal

- When sending direct mail appeals asking for what you consider higher-end gifts ($500 or more), include a handwritten postscript that personalizes your invitation to invest.

Secure Sponsors to Underwrite Direct Mail Appeals

Do you have multiple direct mail appeals throughout the year? Why not get businesses or individuals to sponsor individual appeals or your entire annual package of mailings?

By encouraging businesses or individuals to sponsor an appeal — underwriting its total cost with a gift — you can accomplish several objectives:

- To save needed budget dollars for other worthwhile programs

- To allow the sponsoring donor to see exactly how his/her gift is being used — in this case, to generate more money.

- To provide the sponsor with added visibility: "This mailing underwritten by..."

- To allow greater financial flexibility in creating an attention-grabbing appeal.

HOW TO BOOST PHONATHON RESULTS

In addition to direct mail, telesolicitation provides another way of reaching both past and would-be donors. Your phonathon success will be impacted by factors such as: who makes the call, caller training, the message, timing, funding opportunities and more. Keep testing new and improved approaches with your phonathon: Target a specific group; invite gifts for particular funding projects; test different incentives for giving; compare paid versus volunteer callers; outsource a portion of your list to a telemarketing company and compare results with your in-house efforts.

How to Identify, Attract Volunteer Callers

Many people shy away from fund raising, so it's often challenging to recruit willing phonathon volunteers. To recruit able and willing callers:

1. **Narrow your pool of likely candidates.** Look for people who are outgoing and comfortable with other people. Find people who are connected in some way to your organization and are passionate about its cause.

2. **Offer incentives and proper recognition.** Give gift certificates to the volunteers who receive the largest pledges, the most pledges, etc. Provide a free meal. Recognize them on your website or in publications. Have volunteer hours count toward their school's required community service hours.

3. **Advertise.** Emphasize in meetings, on your website, in newsletters, etc. the need for phonathon volunteers. Use a message like, "Come to meet new people, have fun, eat a delicious meal and raise money for a good cause!"

4. **Eliminate the fear.** Offer training and coaching to help volunteers overcome any calling apprehensions. Provide them with necessary information on the organization and why the funds are being raised, so they feel more comfortable making calls.

> **Attract More Phonathon Volunteers**
>
> Need more volunteer callers willing to step up to the plate? Get someone to donate something of value: a weekend at a resort, an iPhone, a free six-month leased vehicle. Every five completed calls gets the caller one raffle ticket for the prize

Hold a Phonathon on a Shoestring Budget

If your organization is just getting a fundraising program under way, you don't have to be all that sophisticated to initiate your first phonathon. In fact, you can get any associated costs covered with cash and in-kind donations.

To telephone everyone on your mailing list for a first-time contribution, follow these simple steps:

1. Find a business with multiple phone lines willing to donate its bank of phones for a week — during evening hours and over a portion of the weekend. Make sure the contribution includes the business' willingness to pay for long distance phone calls as well.

2. Find another donor or donors willing to underwrite the cost of all printed supplies and postage associated with your phonathon — pledge cards, envelopes, return envelopes, etc.

3. Enlist sufficient numbers of volunteers to fill the designated calling times throughout the duration of your phonathon. Example: Nine phones over five nights and one Sunday afternoon may require about 50 volunteers assuming no one works more than one time.

4. Get a handful of businesses to provide incentive gifts or prizes to award productive volunteer callers and teams (e.g. anyone who lands a pledge for $100 or more; anyone who secures 10 or more pledges).

You don't have to be all that sophisticated to get your first phonathon under way, and you will learn so much from your first event. Most importantly, just do it, and you will see results.

Instruct Callers to Give Specific Reasons to Donate

Whether you use paid callers, volunteers or outsource your telesolicitation procedures, avoid making vague donor requests. Instead, agree to one or more specific projects donors can help support. This simple but important change will help increase donor support dramatically.

Example No. 1 — "Don, this year's phonathon is focused on raising funds for the purchase of 12 to 18 new computers and three new printers for the youth we serve."

Example No. 2 — "Don, this year's phonathon effort is offering you a choice of three important funding projects from which to choose. They include: 1) adding as much as $20,000 more to the Blue & Gold Endowed Scholarship Fund; 2) up to $10,000 for outside lighting; or 3) as much as $40,000 in needed lab equipment. You have the option of directing support to any or all of these projects."

HOW TO BOOST PHONATHON RESULTS

Three Shortcomings Your Phonathon Can't Afford

With some signs that the economy may be turning around, your phonathon has the potential to rebound this year. Just make sure the following everyday issues do not get in the way:

- **A lax phonathon manager.** Is yours headed out the door at 6 o'clock every night, leaving student supervisors in charge too often? That should stop — now. Student supervisors can't replace the real leader of the phonathon — the manager. Jason Fisher (Cedar Rapids, IA), co-author of The Phonathon Manager's Planning Handbook, says, "The faster you realize that, the better off your phonathon will be for it."

- **Insufficient time to reach goals.** Fisher offers this formula for determining how much time you need: Identify the number of completed calls allowing you to achieve a threshold of 70 percent of your database of records. Divide that number by the average completed calls per hour you can expect from the entire program. This will give you the total number of hours needed to achieve 70 percent. Remember to consider the nega-

tive impact that cell phones, caller ID and do-not-call lists may have on your contact rates.

- **A lack of negotiation skills.** "Don't confuse productivity potential with current productivity," says Fisher. One strategy Fisher recommends for improving negotiation is the purchase of a recording device to record calls for training purposes — just check to make sure it's legal in your state. Once you have it, coach calls yourself until you really understand how you want your philosophies taught by your staff. Adjust your scripts according to the reactions you hear from prospects.

One final tip: "Consider awarding prizes based on the quality of the call ... not just the quantity," Fisher says. "Most programs overestimate the quality of their calls. By not addressing this, you're leaving money on the table."

Source: Jason Fisher, Senior Counsel, Advancement Solutions Consulting, A Division of RuffaloCODY, Cedar Rapids, IA. Phone (319) 892-0376. E-mail: Jason.Fisher@ruffalocody.com

Challenge Gift Helps Leverage Phonathon Pledges

Looking for ways to improve your phonathon's results? Secure a challenge gift that callers can include in their pitch.

A challenge gift that will match all new and increased gifts not only helps to leverage giving, it energizes callers as well.

Here's an example of how a challenge gift might be incorporated into a caller's script:

Caller: "I have exciting news to share! One of our agency's board members has established a $50,000 challenge this year. The board

member will match, dollar for dollar, any first-time gifts or any increases over last year of up to $500 per donor.

"According to our records, Bill, you gave $100 last fiscal year. That means our challenger will match any increase you make up to $600 this year. Could you give $600 this year, Bill?"

Even if the person being contacted doesn't give the full ask amount, chances are they will respond to the challenge by making a first-time gift or contributing more than the previous year.

Thorough Solicitation Script Helps Callers Ask for Gifts

To assist volunteers in soliciting annual gifts from their classmates, the office of alumnae/i relations and office of development at Simmons College (Boston, MA) partnered to create a three-page sample script.

The script can be used by callers seeking pledges throughout the year, says Elizabeth Lawton, assistant director for reunion giving, The Simmons Fund.

Created in 2006, the script, which is a part of a leadership guide created for the volunteers, is distributed during the college's Leadership Weekend in October. This event is for all volunteers who give their time and talent to Simmons as class officers, club and regional volunteers, and board members.

The document begins with a simple making-the-ask statement that emphasizes the student caller's important role of encouraging classmates to make gifts to The Simmons Fund through written and personal appeals.

To make it easy for volunteers to use, the script is broken down into sections that follow the natural flow of an ask: introduction; update records; establish rapport; transition/building the case; and confirmation/closing.

The script includes specifics, such as:

- Having the caller identify him/herself as a fellow member of a specific graduating class, mentioning an upcoming reunion and stating that he/she is a class officer.

- Making the case for support that leads into the ask. "We recommend a specific ask for each classmate based on past giving and potential," Lawton says.

- Different scenarios of what could happen on the call are included with tips on how to successfully close a gift.

- Additional tips on how to make fundraising calls and what to expect.

Source: Elizabeth Lawton, Assistant Director for Reunion Giving, The Simmons Fund, Simmons College, Boston, MA. Phone (617) 521-2334. E-mail: Elizabeth.lawton@simmons.edu

> ### Phonathon Comebacks
>
> Here's a script to share next time you come across this common objection to your phonathon request for a gift:
>
> **Prospect: "We just purchased a new home so things are a little tight now."**
>
> Phonathon caller: "Congratulations! Can we get your new address for our records? By the way, just as you'll be able to take advantage of deducting interest payments on your mortgage, you can also deduct your gift to us. Can we count on you for a pledge?"

HOW TO BOOST PHONATHON RESULTS

Survey Helps Monitor Phonathon Callers, Validate Prospects' Opinions

Each year, the annual giving office for Eastern Washington University (Cheney, WA) sends a five-question survey to donors who have pledged through its phonathon. Annual giving officials use the surveys (shown below) to help them recognize outstanding employees and identify areas that need improvement, says Allison Grass, director of annual giving.

"The survey also gives donors a way to provide feedback and show that we value their opinion," Grass says. "Some donors use the form to request information, praise the school and the program, or provide constructive criticism."

Although they haven't tracked whether the surveys have a positive impact on pledge fulfillment, Grass says, she believes that they do. "In addition, the surveys are helpful for building caller morale and for monitoring callers, donor satisfaction and the phonathon itself."

They have been sending the surveys for about five years, she says. They send about 700 per year and receive about 250 back.

Each caller receives a copy of any surveys returned from donors they have brought on board, says Grass. One copy is posted in the calling room for everyone to see, one copy is placed in the caller's personnel file and one copy goes to her.

"I think the callers appreciate receiving the completed surveys," Grass says. "It is also proof to the callers that we are monitoring their calls in a variety of ways and that it is important for them to always be polite, helpful and professional. It is assuring to see that 99.5 percent of the time our donors are very satisfied with their phone experience."

Grass says she is now looking into creating a second survey to send to prospects who decline through the phonathon.

Source: Allison Grass, Assistant Director of Annual Giving, Eastern Washington University, Governor Martin House, Cheney, WA. Phone (509) 359-6525. E-mail: Allison.Grass@mail.ewu.edu

---

Survey Helps Improve Phonathon

Allison Grass, assistant director of annual giving for Eastern Washington University (Cheney, WA), says that for the most part, very few responses they have received via their phonathon donor survey (see story, left) have brought about significant programmatic changes. However, she cites two instances in which they did receive — and act upon — constructive criticism through the surveys:

"The first was that one of our callers is difficult to understand because of her accent," she says. "I spoke with the caller directly, and she is working on speaking slower and enunciating her words more."

The second comment was a little more troubling, says Grass:

"The donor replied 'No!' to the fourth question in the survey, which asked if the student was able to provide answers to their questions while they were on the phone. The donor went on to comment that 'Using brand-new freshman for calls is a bad idea. Student knew nothing about campus life, alumni, traditions, etc.... I was disappointed. Use upperclassman.'

"In five years, this is the first time that I can recall receiving a comment like this," Grass says. "It turns out that the student was indeed a new caller and a freshman. Callers are trained on all of the areas the donor commented about, and they receive reminders and updates about the campus.

"Due to the donor's feedback, we will be paying additional attention to campus education."

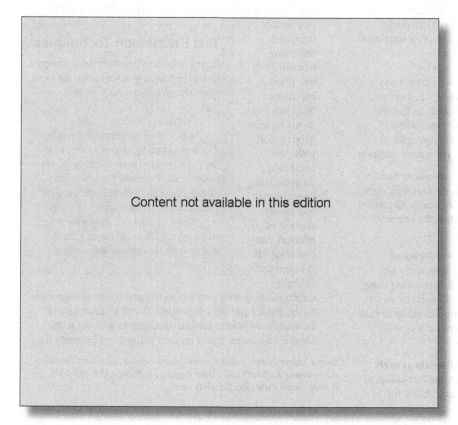

Content not available in this edition

Turn 'Maybe' Into 'Yes'

To help your phonathon callers convert more "maybe" answers into "yes":

1. Offer an incentive to donors who make a firm pledge (e.g., free tickets, inclusion in a drawing for a donated prize, a calendar).
2. Secure a challenge gift that only recognizes pledges.
3. Consider a system in which callers offer to call back a day or two later, after the prospect has had time to think about a pledge.
4. Instruct the caller to hand the phone off to a supervisor standing by and prepared to take those "maybe" calls.

Plan for Phonathon Fill-ins

During your phonathon, have roving staff present to step in for callers who may not know the answers to certain questions.

Having an official join in makes prospects feel special and puts the caller at ease.

HOW TO BOOST PHONATHON RESULTS

Caller Benefits, Prestige Fuel Phonathon

Development staff with Clarkson University (Potsdam, NY) have found the key to success for their annual fund: their annual student phonathon called The Knightline.

The Knightline isn't your average phonathon, says Nichole Thomas, associate director, Clarkson Fund, who notes that Knightline shifts are the most prestigious jobs on campus. In 2007, the phonathon raised more than $689,000.

Thomas recruits students through flyers in student mailboxes, e-mails and recruitment booths at freshman orientation and student activity fairs, and online. Though only 23 spots are available, she aims to recruit 100 students because of natural attrition.

Student callers work two three-hour shifts per week from September to April. In addition to being the highest-paid students on campus, they get free food, work experience, bonuses and incen-

tives, such as gift certificates to local businesses.

Networking opportunities are another incentive, says Thomas, "Some students get offered jobs or internships as a result of connecting with alumni on the phone."

She says the program's greatest benefit is the appreciation it brings from the faculty, staff and president.

"With the exception of one year," she says, "the program has seen nothing but increases since 2003. The formal structure of the Knightline provides recognition of the difference the students make."

Source: Nichole Greene Thomas, Associate Director, Clarkson Fund, Clarkson University, Potsdam, NY. Phone (315) 268-3854. E-mail: ngreene@clarkson.edu

Keep Phonathon Callers Invigorated

To keep calling campaigns alive and productive and callers motivated:

1. **Select a chairperson or co-chairs who are gung ho and will inspire callers.** Enthusiasm is contagious. A determined chairperson will light a fire among callers and keep it lit throughout the calling effort.

2. **Prepare an exciting environment.** Choose a setting with several phones in an open area where callers can see each other at work. Use tote boards listing goals, names of callers and

amount raised to date. Incorporate motivational messages and invite your CEO to stop by and acknowledge callers.

3. **Give callers a reason to do their best.** Tie your telesolicitation effort to a specific funding project rather than a general plea for unrestricted support. Both callers and those being called will respond more enthusiastically.

4. **Incorporate incentives.** Award small prizes to callers who secure pledges. One Midwest college sets up a putting green where successful callers putt for prizes.

Three Ways to Keep Your Phonathon Alive and Thriving

Could the fundraising phonathon soon be a thing of the past?

Jason Fisher, co-author of "The Phonathon Manager's Planning Handbook," says that the phonathon could eventually phase out like any other marketing tool, but rumors of its imminent demise are greatly exaggerated.

"Common sense tells me that until there is a better replacement, phonathon will continue to be the dominant donor retention and acquisition tool in annual fundraising," Fisher says. "However, there are also clear warning signs that tell us that we need to work smarter in the future to keep phonathon relevant."

The phonathon expert suggests the following strategies in order to continue reaping the rewards of a solid phonathon program:

1. **Gather cell phone numbers.** Fisher says institutions that do not focus on gathering cell phone numbers do so at their own peril. "By the end of 2012 it is projected that nearly 33 percent of all households will be wireless only. This is the primary, immediate threat to phonathons in the near future."

2. **Complement phonathon efforts with newer forms of technology.** Today's younger generations rely heavily on texting, instant messaging and online social networking using sites such as Twitter (www.twitter.com) and Facebook (www.facebook.com). Tap into these ways of communicating so that you are able to interact with this population in a way with which they are most comfortable.

3. **Build solid relationships with your constituents as early as possible.** Telephone solicitation is becoming less accepted as time goes on, yet many educational organizations, for

example, still experience great returns because they practice donor education from the first day students are on campus.

Any further legislation restricting telemarketing will greatly hurt those programs that do not establish good rapport with their constituents. To avoid being cast with the less-savory element of telemarketing, Fisher says it is imperative to begin communicating with your supporters and potential supporters today, and not just for solicitation. "It will be necessary to facilitate even greater personal dialogue to increase your chances of moving higher on their philanthropic priority list."

Source: Jason Fisher, Senior Counsel, Advancement Solutions Consulting, A Division of RuffaloCODY, Cedar Rapids, IA. Phone (319) 892-0376. E-mail: Jason.Fisher@ruffalocody.com

---

Test Phonathon Techniques

Just as new direct mail appeal techniques should be tested, you should do the same when phoning individuals for gift support.

Test this procedure:

When phoning previous contributors, instruct one group of callers to ask for a very modest increase over the previous year's gifts. Have the other group of callers ask for a significant increase. Then compare your results.

You may find you get fewer gifts when asking for much larger gifts but end up with far more in gift revenue

---

HOW TO BOOST PHONATHON RESULTS

Reverse Phonathon Offers Alternative Giving Options

Each fall, fundraising professionals with Friends University (Wichita, KS) conduct a reverse phonathon, a direct mail piece giving donors the opportunity to take themselves off the university's phonathon calling list by making a donation.

The fundraiser was originally called a reverse phonathon because persons who gave through the mailing would not receive a telemarketing phone call asking for a donation, says Aaron Winter, director of annual giving. "We've shifted away from this message when promoting our reverse phonathon lately because we don't want to apply a negative connotation to our phonathon."

The reverse phonathon mailing is typically sent annually to the majority of the university's database — nearly 18,000 donors, nondonors, and traditional and non-traditional graduates, Winter says,

noting that they sometimes send the mailing exclusively to donors because their response rate is typically higher than that of nondonors.

The mailing includes a response form allowing donors to mail in their donation. Names of persons who do so are removed from the university's phonathon calling list.

"We usually receive between 500 and 600 gifts, not a very high percentage, but the majority of our database now contains non-traditional graduates who historically do not give as much as traditional graduates," says Winter, who notes the effort is a relatively simple way to raise a large amount of money for a relatively low cost.

Source: Aaron Winter, Director of Annual Giving, Friends University, Wichita, KS. Phone (316) 295-5815. E-mail: winter@friends.edu

10 Tips to Improve Your Callback Rate

Noticing a reduction in number of completed calls or callbacks? Revisit your message and calling methods, says Sylvia Allen, president, Allen Consulting, Inc. (Holmdel, NJ).

"When making telephone calls, you can assume that you will only connect with a maximum of 20 percent of the calls," says Allen. "The rest will be voice mails and this will be your test of talent to get them to return the call."

To leave voice mail messages that will most likely generate a call back, Allen says:

1. Give a reason to return your call. Pique interest with an interesting offer, teaser on a speaker or unique event. For example, "Would you like to meet (name of speaker)? As our partner that can be realized!" Do not give phony offers or unrealistic teasers that would only alienate prospects when they realize they have been misled.

2. Have an objective. Whether it's to get an appointment, make a sale, recruit a volunteer or continue a relationship, keep the objective in mind when making the call.

3. Speak at a moderate speed, clearly identifying yourself and your reason for calling.

4. Remember to breathe as you leave your message to help you keep your pace.

5. Repeat your name and phone number at the beginning and end of each call.

6. Once you have left three messages over a three-day period, don't leave any more. Instead keep dialing day or night until you get a real person.

7. If calling prospects at their place of business, try dialing one number up or down from the number you are calling until you get a real person. Have that person then transfer you to the correct extension.

8. Peak times to reach people are on Fridays between 1 and 3 p.m. and during Christmas and the New Year.

9. Stand up when making calls. "You will have more energy, enthusiasm and passion which is easily transmitted over the phone. It's contagious," says Allen.

10. Practice your techniques by leaving yourself a message. Be objective when you listen. Ask your staff and spouse to listen and offer constructive criticism.

Source: Sylvia Allen, President, Allen Consulting, Inc., Holmdel, NJ. Phone (732) 946-2711. E-mail: Sylvia@allenconsulting.com

Phonathon Caller Tips

- If you reach an answering machine, choose from among these options: 1) mention a day and time you will call back, 2) hold all answering machine calls until the weekend or 3) leave a message that you're sorry you missed them and will send a follow-up letter.

Evaluate Your Phonathon's Success

How do you really know if your phonathon was a winner? Consider each of the following criteria in creating an telesolicitation evaluation instrument:

✓ Did the phonathon reach its goal?

✓ How much was raised from the phonathon as compared to last year's (and previous years') efforts?

✓ What percentage of the total list were callers able to contact?

✓ How many volunteer callers participated?

✓ What was the average size gift raised?

✓ What level of caller training went into the campaign as compared to previous years?

✓ What percentage of donors who pledged actually paid up? What percentage did not?

✓ How many total call attempts were made compared to previous years' efforts?

✓ What percentage of gifts made to the phonathon were from previous nondonors? What was that dollar amount?

✓ What percentage of the previous year's donors increased their level of support? What was the average percentage increase?

✓ How many total caller hours were devoted to calling when compared to previous years?

✓ What were the primary reasons for not contributing to the phonathon?

✓ When asked for their input following the phonathon, what were the key perceptions of your callers? What should be changed in their opinions?

SPECIAL EVENTS WILL ADD TO YOUR BOTTOM LINE

Yes, special events are more labor intensive. No doubt about it. But they also can accomplish what some other forms of fundraising are less effective at doing. Special events can result in gifts from persons and businesses who might not otherwise support your efforts. They reach out to new donors. Special events provide a great opportunity for volunteer involvement and ownership. The publicity surrounding special events brings attention to your organization and importance of gift support. In addition, one successful event can bring in as much as $100,000 in net income and bolster your annual fund totals significantly.

Plan for High Attendance Events

It's no secret that getting donors and prospects to visit your organization builds loyalty, and loyalty results in new and increased gifts.

That being the case, it makes sense to plan events that result in the highest possible attendance. And yet, getting high numbers of attendees can be a real challenge at times.

Whether you're planning on event, such as an anniversary or reunion, or a yearlong series of multiple events, use these strategies and techniques as a way of increasing attendance:

❑ **Involve volunteers early in the planning.** The very act of involving volunteers early in the planning helps to ensure good attendance. If your volunteers are committed, they will be included among the event's attendees. If they are doing their jobs adequately, they will influence others to attend. Based on those assumptions alone, the more volunteers you can legitimately involve in planning and executing the event, the higher your attendance will be. That's why highly structured events are generally well-attended.

❑ **Let your volunteers help shape the event.** Although you will no doubt have a clear vision of what you hope to accomplish through an event and plan to incorporate certain features as a result, it's important to give your volunteers the opportunity to help shape the event and, in so doing, better own it. If it is clear to them what you want to accomplish, they will offer input that complements your goals rather than detracting from them.

❑ **Appeal to multiple interest groups.** Even if you are planning only one event, incorporate different features that appeal to various interest groups. Enlist planning committees for each group as well. An event that appeals to different groups for different reasons is bound to increase overall attendance. Piggybacking is the name of the game!

❑ **Create drawing card appeal.** Incorporate one or more special

features that make the event special or unique. Such features might include: a celebrity who will be present, a momentous public announcement, well-known entertainment, etc. Such a feature helps set your event apart from all others.

❑ **Let others know who will be there.** If your constituency knows one another, as in the case of college or university alumni, it may be helpful to publicize (in advance) those who have said they plan to attend. The excitement of seeing friends who plan to attend will encourage others to attend.

❑ **Incorporate tangible benefits for attending.** Beyond the social or altruistic reasons for attending, incorporate tangible benefits for attending the event (e.g. continuing education credits, useful seminars, a certificate of recognition of appreciation, etc.)

❑ **Consider the special needs of your attendees.** Who are you most hoping to attract, and what would make them more likely to attend? If, for example, you want to encourage family attendance, child care and activities for youth may provide special incentive. If, on the other hand, you are reaching out to senior citizens, issues like accessibility to facilities and physical comfort may take on greater meaning. Volunteer committee members can help to identify these special features that demonstrate attention to detail.

❑ Conduct a post-event evaluation. Meet with committee members and staff soon after the event's completion to review the strengths and weaknesses of it. In addition, send a simple survey to attendees (if appropriate) asking for their perceptions of the event. Be sure to record the results of the evaluation for future reference and planning.

As much time as it takes to plan any event, it's worth your while to plan the right way from the very beginning. And if attendance builds to loyalty and loyalty helps increase giving, why not focus on events that burst at the seams?

Watching the Pennies: Creating an Event Budget

When creating a budget for your next event, follow this checklist for properly accounting for and tracking expenses:

❑ Work closely with your caterer to determine food and beverage costs. Don't forget to build in the cost of gratuity of the wait staff, which can be up to 20 percent above and beyond the caterer's total.

❑ If your event will require equipment rental, note all fees and build a cushion for breakage costs and late fees.

❑ Itemize cost of gifts for guests, staff and/or volunteers. No matter how economical the gift, costs can add up because of number of items purchased.

❑ Calculate cost of transportation to include shuttles that may be provided to guests, as well as driver tips.

❑ When choosing the event site, obtain a bid from at least three potential sites to determine the best value. Build in extra for costs associated with early set-up and tear-down of the event.

❑ If you're holding your event outdoors, account for tent, table, chair and bathroom facility rental.

❑ Allow for a contingency fund. Estimate approximately 10 to 20 percent of your total to a contingency fund that allows for extras that were overlooked.

❑ Summarize your costs and review them again. Look meticulously for areas in which you can pare back to save expense without compromising guest comfort or the quality of your event.

48

SPECIAL EVENTS WILL ADD TO YOUR BOTTOM LINE

Managing Event Costs in a Crisis Economy

A troubled economy can mean trouble for your organization's next big event. Fewer people may attend, and those who do may spend less.

Lori Stachnik, Lori Stachnik Events (Amsterdam, NY) says the following tips can offset those losses by controlling the costs of your event.

✓ **Get creative with décor.** Ask all florists in town to donate one or two centerpieces for the event, and then auction them off at the end of the night. Make sure to give the florists a color scheme or common theme so the various pieces still work together. Another way to get creative with the décor, especially if your organization serves children or young people, is to get clients involved with making centerpieces.

✓ **Offer a sit-down dinner.** Many people are surprised to find a sit-down meal actually costs less than the alternatives. Stachnik says that's because you have to buffer the cost of buffets and food stations to avoid the risk of running out of

anything. A sit-down dinner also allows the caterers to have portion control so they can offer a cheaper per-person price. Switching your event to off-peak times of the year can help reduce costs, too.

✓ **Cut back on the bar.** Limit open bar to the first hour or just offer wine on the table with dinner. If you opt for the latter, Stachnik says it's possible to get the wine donated to cut that cost completely.

✓ **Get into the spirit of the season.** Stachnik says you can get inexpensive décor items to stretch your decorating dollar by going seasonal (e.g., in autumn make the most of hay bales, cornstalks, pumpkins, leaves, etc.). Scour dollar and discount stores to find dirt-cheap items to create room and table décor. If the event will have a similar theme next year, make sure to scoop up bargains at post-holiday sales.

Source: Lori Stachnik, Lori Stachnik Events, Amsterdam, NY. Phone (518) 843-6885.

Use Checklist to Make Events More Manageable

Special event planning can seem overwhelming. With the date growing steadily nearer and the to-do list growing longer, how will you ever get everything accomplished by the big day?

Don't become paralyzed by the feeling of not knowing where to begin. Rather, put pen to paper today and develop a checklist that you can either share with others or use yourself to track and monitor event planning progress. Doing so will make the tasks and many deadlines seem much more manageable.

Here's how to create an effective checklist for your next event:

1. **Start making a list.** Begin by thinking about and listing everything you can imagine that will need to be done, regardless of who is responsible for doing it. List both big-picture items and details — whatever comes to mind. Don't get caught up in prioritizing items or worrying about the order of things at this point. Carry your checklist around and keep adding items as they come to mind.

2. **Review your list and assign individual checklist items to appropriate categories.** As you develop a list of everything you can imagine that will need to happen at some point along the way, the entire event — from start to finish — will become more clear in your mind. You can now begin to group individual actions into common categories (e.g., invitations and ticket sales, sponsorships, hospitality, program, location and so on). The completion

of these groupings helps to provide a big-picture view of the project and points out gaps among actions that will need to occur. Fill these gaps with additional needed checklist items.

3. **Assign deadlines and persons responsible for each checklist item.** Once your checklist is relatively complete (you'll probably keep adding details as you think of them), organize your list by category and chronologically. Assign a deadline date to each checklist item along with names of persons responsible for seeing it happens. This process will help you transform your checklist into a timetable as well.

The creation of an event checklist will help you better visualize what needs to take place from start to finish and also helps to keep you and others on track. Use this example to get started on your own:

Checklist for May 23, 2011 Special Event

Action Item	Responsible Persons	Deadline	Action Item	Responsible Persons	Deadline
PRE-EVENT			**DURING EVENT**		
☐ Select program speaker	Gard	10/10/10	☐ Take tickets	Marcus	5/23
☐ Enlist project committee	Gard	1/3/11	☐ Handle general and		
☐ Schedule regular			special seating	Holt	5/23
committee meetings	Gard	1/8	☐ Oversee meal	Holt	5/23
☐ Cmte. members recruit			☐ Oversee music and		
sub-committee members	Holt/Wen	1/22	sound system	Holt	5/23
☐ Planning meeting	Gard	1/23	☐ Host speaker	Gard	5/23
☐ Decide on location	Holt	2/4	☐ Seat head table	Gard	5/23
☐ Design invitations	Wen	3/14	☐ Event publicity	Wen	5/23
☐ Send invitations	Wen	5/6			
☐ Conduct publicity			**POST EVENT**		
for the effort	Wen	5/10	☐ Speaker to airport	Gard	5/23
☐ Place advertising	Wen	5/6	☐ Clean-up crew	Holt	5/23
☐ Design & print program	Wen	5/6	☐ Follow-up correspondence	Gard	5/27
☐ Sell tickets — individual			☐ Evaluate event	Gard	6/11
or tables of 10	Marcus	4/14	☐ Pick date for next year	All	6/11
☐ Decorate facility	Holt	5/22			
☐ Order sound system	Holt	2/4			
☐ Arrange for head table	Gard	5/7			

SPECIAL EVENTS WILL ADD TO YOUR BOTTOM LINE

Assigning Co-chairs Can Boost Event Success

The Nightingale Ball — the annual fundraising gala for the Ojai Valley Community Hospital Foundation Guild (Ojai, CA) — requires significant planning and organization to ensure event success.

In its seventh year, the event owes much of its success to the tradition of naming event co-chairs rather than relying on a single person to head the event.

Nita Whaley, guild member and former co-chair, says the co-chair structure offers necessary support to those in charge while contributing to a more diverse and creative approach to managing the event.

Nightingale Ball's co-chairs often have been a husband/wife team who shoulder the responsibilities of organizing the event by drawing on each other's talents. Whaley co-chaired the 2007 event with her husband, Don Anderson.

A successful co-chair structure involves having the board appoint a team willing to chair an event together — a husband and wife or any other two people who have been instrumental in the organization. The co-chairs then determine which tasks they are best suited to fulfill and assign subcommittee roles to guild members who are willing to lend a hand.

Whaley recommends appointing co-chairs based on the following qualities:

❑ Consider candidates' past level of involvement and willingness to take charge.

❑ Select persons who demonstrated a high level of commitment to the organization.

❑ Select co-chairs who will follow through and generate support.

In the case of the Nightingale Ball, co-chairs are frequently retirees able to devote additional time to organizing the event, which can span an entire year. The ball averages 225 guests each year and has raised more than $500,000 for the nonprofit hospital.

"Having co-chairs is a definite plus in recruiting candidates and certainly makes the job easier," says Whaley. "But the enthusiasm, hard work and follow-through of the entire volunteer team are equally vital to the event's success."

Source: Nita Whaley, Ojai Guild Board Member, Ojai Hospital, Ojai, CA. Phone (805) 640-2317. E-mail: crock@ojaihospital.org

Fundraising in a Soft Economy: Gamble and Gain Big

With the economy in a slump, staff and supporters of Aid for AIDS of Nevada (AFAN), Las Vegas, NV, knew they would have to take drastic steps to make the organization's popular — but highly unconventional — Black & White Party a success.

By making three significant changes, they found out that not playing it safe could pay off big. How big? AFAN saw a 57 percent jump in attendance and $40,000 boost in revenue for the 2009 event compared to 2008, just by making a few simple changes.

Popular Event Grows From Barbecue to Sophisticated Soiree

The Black & White Party started 23 years ago as a backyard, pool side birthday party for two men who requested that, in lieu of gifts, invitees bring canned goods to donate to AFAN. As the guest list has grown, the party has moved to bigger and better locations, morphing from a simple barbecue to a decadent sampling of foods from 13 of the finest restaurants in the city and spirits from nine vendors.

However, attire remains the same: black and white.

"The black-and-white attire and theme really came from the barcodes on the (donated food) cans," says Jennifer Morss, AFAN executive director. "Of course, now with 2,800 people attending the party, we've had to discontinue accepting canned goods, because it's just too much to deal with, but we've always kept the theme the same."

Fresh Venue, Cheaper Tickets, Networking Boost Bottom Line

So what helped make the 2009 event such an overwhelming success? A fresh venue, lower ticket prices and using social networking to spread the word.

"We knew that with the economy what it was and with this being a more unconventional fundraiser, we had to do something to generate a higher attendance," Morss says. "It's a party, not a family event, and that already makes it harder to secure corporate sponsorships. We started by lowering ticket prices because it's much easier to spend $35 than it is to spend $50 right now. We also knew that we needed to come up with a different venue. We'd been at our old venue for five years and it was time to move on."

With a generous donation of space, security, staff and product from the Hard Rock Café Las Vegas (in exchange for a promise from AFAN to sell a block of rooms at a discounted rate) and with the lowered ticket prices, sales skyrocketed.

While Morss and her colleagues were pleased, she says they were also a bit surprised: "We didn't expect this kind of turnout.... We had hoped to raise at least $80,000, but to hit $120,000 was just amazing. As a bonus, we sold out the Hard Rock — even their new tower that they just opened."

Shift From Print to Electronic Media Kicks Up Attendance

Morss and staff did the majority of their marketing via social media. All ticket sales were done online and billboards were digital as well. They used social media sites like Facebook and Twitter to promote ticket sales and offer additional discounts to fans.

"We promised a lot of marketing for in-kind donations as well," Morss adds. "We have a database of 30,000 people, so we promised a lot of exposure for any companies willing to donate funds or materials. And with e-blasts going out every other week in the months before the event, and then every week the month of the event, we feel that we lived up to our promise."

Source: Jennifer Morss, Executive Director, Aid for AIDS of Nevada, Las Vegas, NV. Phone (702)382-2326. E-mail: Jennifer@afanlv.org

---

Special Event Tips

- To help pre-sell tickets and recognize past attendees, give the previous year's participants a chance to buy tickets before a specified date.

- Make planning your special event a special experience for your committee. Incorporate portions of your event into the planning process.

- Develop strategies to sell 78 percent of the event's tickets prior to sending invitations.

- Select an event that appeals to your constituency and is consistent with their pocketbooks.

SPECIAL EVENTS WILL ADD TO YOUR BOTTOM LINE

A Winning Bet: Casino Parties

An odds-on favorite party is one with casino games that boost fundraising or just add to the fun. For yours to be a success, don't gamble on the outcome — heed these tips from Crystal Clarke, customer services manager, All Star Productions (Arlington, TX):

✓ **Offer prizes.** "A successful casino party always has something for people to look forward to at the end, whether a raffle, drawing or an auction," Clarke says. "When the guests don't have an incentive to actually play the games, they're not as excited."

✓ **Include the favorites.** Be sure to have black-jack tables, "a very simple game that 90 percent of the people understand," Clarke says. Roulette is also easy to learn, and craps, while more complicated, is typically the highest-energy game and can really get the crowd going. Texas Hold 'em is popular, although since players are betting against each other and not the house, it's tough to amass many chips for prizes.

✓ **Don't assume everyone will want to play.** Plan enough gambling spots for 70 percent of attendees. Offer other entertainment, such as video arcade arena, dancing and a DJ who can also make announcements and entertain non-gamblers.

✓ **Institute a maximum bet.** "This keeps things fair on all the tables, especially when you're giving prizes," Clarke says. It also helps prevent a shortage of chips, a definite party downer. A max bet of $2,000 to $5,000 is standard.

✓ **If hiring an outside company, get questions answered beforehand.** A company's quote should include setup and tear-down, dealers, a pit boss and all tools necessary to play the games. The pit boss should walk around and be a liaison with both you and the dealers. You should offer water and sodas to the staff working the party, but you should never be expected to provide food. Most casino parties last about three hours and seem to fizzle out after that, but discuss beforehand cost for extra time if the party goes late.

Source: Crystal Clarke, Customer Services Manager, All Star Productions, Arlington, TX. Phone (214) 642-6468.
E-mail: crystal@allstarproductions.net

Poker Event Serves Up a Full House

The Showdown for St. Louis Arc Texas Hold 'Em Tournament is a fundraising smash. In its fifth year, the annual event at St. Louis Arc (St. Louis, MO) draws 130 guests and raises $25,000 to support the nonprofit's programs that support those with developmental disabilities with pertinent services, family support and advocacy.

The organization trains 35 dealers to entertain guests at 17 tables for the one-night affair. Organizers offer tips on how to plan a successful poker event:

• **Find expert dealer trainers.** Contact a local casino or organization that will train your dealers as a volunteer effort toward your event.

• **Pre-train dealers.** One week prior to the annual poker event, event organizers at St. Louis Arc bring together experienced dealers from previous events and trainees for a night of learning. Dealers learn the basics of dealing a poker game, plus style and finesse for card handling. This training is mandatory for all dealers at the St. Louis Arc event and ensures that dealers are ready to fulfill their task at the tables.

• **Pair new dealers with experienced dealers.** Pairing dealers is an excellent way to introduce new dealers to your event. Having an experienced dealer sidekick allows new dealers a level of comfort and an opportunity to share the role while learning. Pairing also ensures that rules are followed.

• **Tap local businesses and young professional groups when recruiting new dealers for the event.** St. Louis Arc considers local businesses and young professional groups when seeking the right personalities for dealers of the evening. Look to seasoned volunteers to become pit bosses for the event. Pit bosses must be fluent with the rules of poker and intervene when rules are questioned.

Source: Audrey Ting, Coordinator of Volunteers and Community Outreach, and Lindsey Harris, Special Events Manager, St. Louis Arc, St. Louis, MO. Phone (314) 569-2211. E-mail: ATing@slarc.org or LHarris@slarc.org

The reply card, left, and flyer for the Texas Hold 'Em Poker Tournament for the St. Louis Arc (St. Louis, MO), emphasize the event's theme.

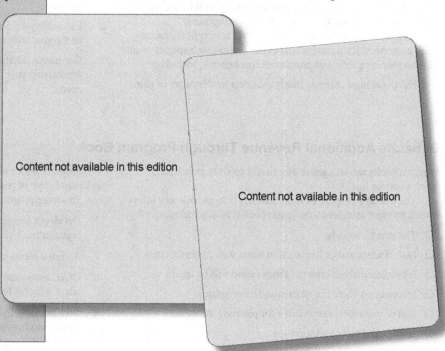

Content not available in this edition

Content not available in this edition

SPECIAL EVENTS WILL ADD TO YOUR BOTTOM LINE

Motorcycle Riders Cruise to Victory in Fundraising Efforts

You might not think that motorcycle riders and sick children go together, but George S. Wilson, one of the organizers of the Cruise Motorcycle Benefit Ride for the Ronald McDonald House (Rochester, MN) says you couldn't be more wrong.

"The riders might look rough in some cases, but they have hearts of gold and would do anything for the kids who are going through treatments and staying at the Ronald McDonald House," Wilson says.

That might explain why the biker-driven event has raised more than $500,000 in the last eight years and grown to become the largest motorcycle benefit ride in southern Minnesota.

Here's how the cruise works: A committee of 12 to 15 volunteers begins work 10 months before the annual event to plan the route, solicit donations and make arrangements. Those arrangements include selecting stops along the 132-mile ride, arranging food at those stops, coordinating a live and silent auction and planning a parade that goes from the ride's end point, Rochester Community College, to the Ronald McDonald House.

The committee also secures the necessary permits for the parade and business sponsors at two different levels: $1,000 and $2,500.

Event day starts very early with 30 to 40 volunteers handling registration, staging the auctions, placing sponsor banners and checking microphones and other equipment to make sure everything is ready for the big day.

Wilson says that the committee changes the route every year to keep interest up among the riders, but that it's really the parade and the chance to meet with the children at the house that keep them coming back.

Following the parade, organizers present an oversized check to children at the Ronald McDonald House.

The 2009 event included 1,280 riders — many of whom participate each year — and raised $124,000, helping offset the house's operating budget by 10 percent.

Source: George S. Wilson, Rochester, MN.
Phone (507) 288-3834.
E-mail: gewilson@
heartman-insurance.com

At a Glance —	
Event Type:	Motorcycle benefit ride and parade
Gross:	$120,000-plus
Costs:	$8,000-9,000
Net Income:	$110,000-plus
Volunteers:	12 on committee; 30-40 more on event day
Planning:	10 months
Attendees:	1,200-plus
Revenue Sources:	Rider registration, sponsorships and T-shirt sales
Use of funds:	Operating budget for Ronald McDonald House of Rochester, MN
Unique Feature:	Largest motorcycle benefit ride in southern Minnesota

Partner With Another Nonprofit for Mutually Profitable Event

Looking for a way to generate $10,000 or more in new funds? Partner with another nonprofit with a mission different from your own to organize a joint fundraising event that will benefit both organizations equally, both in added funds and added exposure.

People love to see collaboration among nonprofit organizations, even when it's a fundraising event. Cohosting a special event with another nonprofit will provide mutual benefits, including:

1. Having at least twice as much volunteer involvement in planning and coordinating the event — maybe more if additional nonprofits are involved — making the event a bit less labor intensive.

2. Exposing your nonprofit to attendees who might not otherwise be familiar with or support your efforts.

3. Generating additional needed funds to help meet your annual fundraising goal or support a special project or immediate need.

Generate Additional Revenue Through Program Book

Program books can be a great way to add profit to your special event's bottom line.

The primary purpose of such booklets is to provide key information to event attendees. A program book typically includes:

❑ The event's agenda.

❑ List of silent and/or live auction items with minimum bids.

❑ Information about how the funds raised will be used.

❑ Information about the charity and its programs.

❑ List of volunteers responsible for planning the event.

❑ Names of donors and sponsors.

Program books may also include paid advertisements that help underwrite costs of producing the books and raise additional funds. To secure program book ad income:

1. Develop a simple letter and ad form to send to your organization's vendors.

2. Assign a separate committee to call on businesses for ads.

3. Offer discounted or free event tickets for those who purchase ads at a higher level.

4. Give prizes to those volunteers selling ads based on dollars and/or numbers of ads generated.

SPECIAL EVENTS WILL ADD TO YOUR BOTTOM LINE

Securing Key Sponsors Helps Golf Event Mark Record Year

Staff with Kaplan University (Fort Lauderdale, FL) has organized a successful golf tournament for five consecutive years, including this year, in which the event raised a record $30,000 for three South Florida nonprofit organizations.

Sponsorships of all levels make the event a success.

"No sponsorship is too small. Every dollar counts and makes a difference," says Sherry Thompson, manager of events and community outreach. "It's important to us that the net proceeds from the tournament go directly to the benefiting organizations, and we always ensure that enough dollars are collected to provide each nonprofit with an equal dollar amount."

To help maximize event proceeds, organizers create a detailed list of expenses they will incur to create the most accurate budget possible, says Thompson, noting that the list also allows event planners to identify ways sponsors can contribute to the event.

Such budget items include course fees; insurance; putting contest and raffle prizes; tourney shirts; signage fees (including directional signage); parking; printed materials; and items for the goodie bags.

Organizing sponsors to donate funds to cover the above items is a great way to offset costs, Thompson says, noting that this year's event yielded the highest sponsorship participation for its golf tournament to date — a total of 18 sponsors.

Beyond platinum, gold and silver sponsorship levels, event organizers include sponsorship levels for the putting contest ($2,500), pin sponsors ($1,500), goodie bag sponsors ($500) and table sponsors ($100).

Thompson offers advice for securing sponsors for your next golf event:

1. **Start early.** Kaplan organizers plan a year in advance of the tourney to maximize sponsorship dollars, contacting sponsors seven or more times during the year.

2. **Establish a budget.** For instance, organizers of the Kaplan event set a goal for how much they want to donate to charity, then figure out how to raise the money to cover the donation and the tournament costs and how many sponsors will be needed.

3. **Compose a formal sponsorship letter detailing levels of sponsorship.** Offer sponsorship levels that are creative and specifically cover costs such as the goodie bag expenses (see letter, right).

Source: Sherry Thompson, Manager of Events and Community Outreach, Linnea Brown, Senior Public Relations Associate, Kaplan University, Fort Lauderdale, FL. Phone (954) 515-3651. E-mail: LBrown3@kaplan.edu

The sponsorship letter for an annual golf tourney hosted by Kaplan University (Fort Lauderdale, FL) spells out various sponsor levels along with their associated benefits.

Employees Direct Tourney Proceeds

For five years, Kaplan University (Fort Lauderdale, FL) has put on a highly successful golf tournament. Proceeds support three South Florida nonprofits: Children's Home Society of Florida Intercoastal Division, Children's Home Society South Coastal Division and the Urban League of Broward County.

With nearly 80 percent of the 200 tournament participants also Kaplan University employees, it makes sense that they take part in selecting the area charities that benefit from the proceeds, says Sherry Thompson, manager of events and community outreach.

"When Kaplan University opened its online student support center in Fort Lauderdale in 2005, it invited employees to help select the community nonprofit organizations it would partner with," Thompson says. "Employees selected three that place significant emphasis on education and mentorship, and Kaplan has remained committed to supporting those organizations each year since."

In choosing the recipient organizations, she says, a panel of management and staff considered a number of local organizations, identifying three nonprofits that most closely align with Kaplan's educational goals. The finalists went through executive review, where they gained approval.

Content not available in this edition

SPECIAL EVENTS WILL ADD TO YOUR BOTTOM LINE

Auction Doubles Attraction With Bachelor Dates, Event Packages

An event that began as a former board member's idea has grown from a small gathering to a signature fundraiser for a Florida nonprofit.

In its seventh year, the Bachelor, Baskets and Services Auction to benefit the Community Service Council of West Pasco (New Port Richey, FL) combines the auctioning of dates with local bachelors with service packages to appeal to a wide variety of attendees.

"We have single women (or groups of women or offices) looking to buy a bachelor for themselves or single friends," says Becky Bennett, special events chair. "With the service packages, married and not-single women can come for the show of auctioning off the bachelors and still purchase great service packages. Even men come to this event and bid on service items."

This year, organizers put 13 bachelors and 12 service packages on the auction block. Funds raised go to scholarships for high school seniors, one adult scholarship and other projects the council does to benefit the community.

The bachelors ranged in age from 29 to 50-something and offered prospective bidders a wide selection of dates, including:

✓ Dinner and a comedy club.

✓ Kayaking, lunch and ice cream.

✓ Double date in a limo to a yacht ride followed by dinner, sunset cruise and dancing.

✓ Drinks at sunset from a balcony followed by a candlelit dinner, moonlit walk at the pier on the gulf, drinks and music at a local club.

The 12 service packages, each with a minimum value of $500, included:

✓ An enchanted evening package featuring a couples massage.

✓ A personal chef preparing a Couples Aphrodisiacs' Dinner at either the chef's restaurant or the couple's home.

✓ A pig-out and party package featuring a dinner for eight provided by a local barbecue restaurant and four hours of DJ service.

✓ A getaway package packed with a four-hour fishing trip, a round of golf for four at a local country club, two-month membership and 50 percent off group weight-training classes at the YMCA.

Bennett says the 2009 event raised a record $19,250. Bids on bachelors raised more than $4,000; service packages, $3,600; sponsorships, more than $5,900; ticket sales, $2,600; 50/50 raffle and Chinese auction, $2,000; diamond and ruby ring live auction, $410.

Source: Becky Bennett, Special Events Chair, Community Service Council of West Pasco, Hudson, FL.
Phone (727) 967-7509.
E-mail:
bbennetthfpasco@aol.com

At a Glance —	
Event Type:	Bachelor & Services Auction
Gross:	$19,250
Costs:	$3,050
Net Income:	$16,200
Volunteers:	40-plus
Planning:	3 months
Attendees:	250
Revenue Sources:	Sponsorships, ticket sales, bachelor and service package auctions, live auction, 50/50 raffle, Chinese auction tickets
Unique Feature:	Offers dual attraction of bidding on dates with bachelors as well as couple and group-oriented outings

Seek Ways to Improve Event Each Year

To build on success, organizers of the Bachelor, Baskets and Services Auction for the Community Service Council of West Pasco (New Port Richey, FL) look for ways to improve the event year to year.

This year, for example, they put the auction stage in the middle of the room to give all bidders a good view and equal chance to bid on dates.

They also extended the beginning of the evening when guests could mingle and get acquainted with the gentlemen who agreed to put themselves up on the block.

Add Online Component to Your Next Fundraising Auction

When preparing for your next live or silent auction event, consider adding a new component to increase sales: an online auction.

The advantage to adding this online option is that it allows those who support your cause and/or have interest in the items up for bid but are unable to attend the opportunity to bid. This, in turn, can result in significantly higher final bids and a better overall result for your auction-driven event.

To generate additional interest in your auction, offer items online that will not be available at the live or silent auction portion of the event. This will significantly increase your earnings potential and may get online bidders to also attend your special event.

SPECIAL EVENTS WILL ADD TO YOUR BOTTOM LINE

Firefly Art Fair Draws Crowd, Funds

For 23 years, the Wauwatosa Historical Society (Wauwatosa, WI) has hosted its Firefly Art Fair, and organizers say the years of experience have paid off. Grossing nearly $35,000 and averaging 5,000 attendees each year, this event has grown to be the historical society's largest fundraiser.

In 2009, more than 90 artists participated in the event by renting outdoor booth space on the historical site's 1.5-acre grounds. Art fair attendees go from booth to booth to view artists' original works, walk through the site's Victorian gardens and visit the historic Kneeland-Walker House. Intermixed throughout the grounds are food vendors who offer homemade pie, sandwiches and beverages, including beer, while live music plays in the background.

The event raises funds from its ticket sales, silent auction featuring original works donated by participating artists, food and beverage sales and artist booth rental fees.

Janel Ruzicka, the historical society's executive director, offers advice from the seasoned event planners of the 23rd Annual Firefly Art Fair for making similar events successful:

✓ *Consider the economic climate.* After careful consideration, the Firefly Art Fair event planners did not raise their food prices in 2009 even though the cost of the food went up. Additionally, artist fees and ticket pricing remained the same as the previous year to continue to draw a large crowd.

✓ *Ignore the weather.* Ruzicka recommends holding the event rain or shine. When rain falls, she says, attendees actually tend to huddle under vendor tents and buy more items from each vendor in gratitude for the cover.

✓ *Create a pleasant atmosphere for guests.* Offer a variety of options for the guests, from artists booths to historic venue and great food. The Firefly Art Fair prides itself on offering homemade, down-home foods appealing to guests.

✓ *Create a pleasant atmosphere for visiting artists.* Treat artists with the utmost respect. At this art fair, artists are treated to a Saturday evening artist reception and a Sunday morning breakfast.

✓ *Persistence is key.* In the first years of offering an art fair, Ruzicka recommends not building profits into your budget. Also, she says, expect to offer an event such as this for two to three years without gains. Longevity, consistency and building your reputation are the keys to turning an art fair into a significant fundraiser.

Source: Janel Ruzicka, Executive Director, Wauwatosa Historical Society, Kneeland-Walker House & Gardens, Wauwatosa, WI. Phone (414) 774-8672. E-mail: staff@ wauwatosahistoricalsociety.org

At a Glance —	
Event Type:	Art Fair
Gross:	$35,000
Costs:	$3,000
Net Income:	$32,000
Volunteers:	100
Planning:	12 months
Attendees:	5,000
Revenue Sources:	Admission fees ($4); food and beverage sales; silent auction; artist booth rental
Unique Features:	Artists pay booth rental to sell art; venue is a historic house open for viewing during art fair

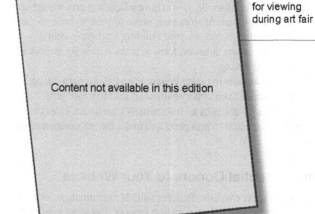

Content not available in this edition

Special Event Follow Up

Special events help to broaden your base of support. They create relationships where none may have previously existed. That's why it's important to take crucial follow-up steps after a completed fundraising event.

Send personal thank-you letters to everyone who attended and may have also given in other ways: purchased auction items, served as sponsors, purchased a raffle ticket and more. Acknowledge those acts in your letter of thanks.

Don't allow a special event to turn into a one-time connection. Use that opportunity to forge relationships with all attendees.

RAISE MORE ANNUAL GIFTS VIA YOUR WEBSITE, E-MAIL

Increasing numbers of nonprofit organizations are realizing significant gift revenue via their websites and e-appeal efforts. And without printing and postage costs, the net return can be significantly better than direct mail efforts. What are you doing to make your website more donor friendly? In what ways are you driving traffic to your website? Are you becoming more proactive with e-appeal efforts to targeted segments of your database?

How to Integrate Fundraising Into Your Website

When developing a website, to integrate your fundraising and over-all strategic plan, says Michel Hudson, owner of 501(c)onsulting (Round Rock, TX).

"Your annual fundraising and major gift campaigns can all be integrated into your website as a way to get people excited about your programs," Hudson says. "One way to do that is to integrate your donor/prospect database into your online e-mail newsletter sign-up function so that visitors who sign up for your e-newsletter are automatically added to your prospect database."

Hudson shares additional ways to integrate fundraising into your website:

- Include links throughout your electronic solicitations to direct donors and prospects to additional information on your website.
- Make sure you have consistent branding in print and online pieces so donors always know the source of information.
- Be sure to always make an ask, whether it is to respond to calls for action, become a member or donate to your programs.
- Use your website to highlight specific campaign projects or programs. For example, if you have a building project, set up a Web cam and include streaming video to your website so that your constituents can see your building's progress online.
- Include an online donation form to make it easy for donors to renew their giving.
- Use your website to create volunteer and social networking opportunities. Such opportunities can lead to major gifts.
- Set up your website as an information warehouse. Use it to push information to prospects and make the information easier

to access. For example, putting information online eliminates printing costs for annual reports and research reports. Online technology also provides dynamic, interesting options for delivering information.

- Show progress reports online so that donors can see where their money is going. This also makes it easy for them to see the successes your organization is having and grow more confident about supporting it.

Source: Michel Hudson, Owner, 501(c)onsulting, Round Rock, TX. Phone (512) 565-0142. E-mail: mhudson@501consulting.com

---

Nonprofit Website Dos and Don'ts

Michel Hudson, owner of 501(c)onsulting (Round Rock, TX), shares steps not to take when developing your nonprofit website:

✓ Don't include a What's New box if you're not going to update it regularly. You should update a What's New box at least monthly.

✓ Don't make members e-mail you to subscribe to your e-newsletter or other updates. Create an automatic process for joining or subscribing to those features.

✓ Don't refer to links that aren't active.

✓ Don't post a thermometer or other gauge of fundraising progress until you raise at least 50 percent of your goal. If your goal is $1 million and your thermometer says you have raised $1,000, prospective donors will think your fundraising has not been successful.

Drive Potential Donors to Your Website

Your organization's website features valuable information, as well as an easy and secure online donation process. But what good is the site without traffic?

Here are six ways to drive potential donors to your organization's website:

1. **Encourage referrals.** Include a refer-a-friend option on your website letting visitors send an e-mail to friends suggesting they check out your website (we all know a friend's suggestion truly means something!) Consider the same option for your e-newsletter.

2. **Be a tease.** If your organization does not have a blog, start one. Blogs are a great way to share your message. To get people to visit your site, entice them with a teaser. For instance, if your website features informational articles, post the first few lines on your blog, along with a link to your website to read the rest of the story.

3. **YouTube.** Ask a local college to help make a short video or develop a video campaign to post on YouTube. Be sure to check out YouTube's nonprofit program (www.youtube.com/nonprofits) and create your own channel. When making the video mention or show your organization's Web address several times.

4. **Offer incentives.** Give people a reason to visit your site. For instance, encourage persons to register for a drawing. Or, pose a question or quiz in your newsletter with directions to visit your website for the answer.

5. **Trade links.** Ask other nonprofit organizations or event sponsors to include a link to your website from theirs. Don't forget to ask that CEO on your board of directors to post a link on his/her company site.

6. **Apply for a Google Grant** (www.google.com/grants). Recipients receive at least three months of free advertising up to $10,000 per month. As a recipient, you'll choose keywords relevant to your organization. When Google users search for those keywords, your AdWords ad will appear. Users can click on the ad and go directly to your organization's website.

Online Giving Tip

- To encourage immediate contributions, have a GIVE NOW button on your website's home page and as many other pages as you can justify.

RAISE MORE ANNUAL GIFTS VIA YOUR WEBSITE, E-MAIL

What Donors Expect From Your Website

Donors have certain expectations when visiting your website, says Michel Hudson, owner of 501(c)onsulting (Round Rock, TX): "Donors want to feel connected to your organization and as though they are part of your family. They also want to know that you have similar outlooks and objectives to theirs."

To fulfill those donor expectations, says Hudson:

- **Have compelling website copy.** Your text needs to compel them to donate, participate in a call to action and/or read more about your organization. It should inform people about your cause, what you are doing and how they can help.

- **Tell them where the money goes.** This makes them feel confident about your cause.

- **Share your research and any results, insights or successes.**

People want to know more about what interests them and that's why they are coming to your site.

- **Make it easy and secure for visitors to make donations.** You want to limit the number of steps it takes to get to the donation.

- **Include a prominent and well-stated privacy policy.**

- **Make sure website content is fresh.** This gives donors confidence in your organization. "Be aware that search engine optimization is based on freshness," Hudson notes. "The more your content changes, the higher rankings you will get with search engines. But don't change things just for change — make it meaningful."

Source: Michel Hudson, Owner, 501(c)onsulting, Round Rock, TX. Phone (512) 565-0142. E-mail: mhudson@501consulting.com

Social Networking as a Fundraising Tool: Myths vs. Realities

To innovate the approach to fundraising, St. Olaf College (Northfield, MN) has joined the universe of social networking. St. Olaf can be found on Twitter, Facebook, Myspace, and LinkedIn. In addition, St. Olaf reunion volunteers have created class-specific groups and fan pages to promote their reunions.

Matt Fedde, associate director of annual giving, answers questions on what social networking means for higher education fundraising:

Why did you decide to try social networking as a fundraising tool?

"We thought, 'all good online social networking is free, so why not?' The decision to get involved was easy and so was creating the accounts. The tricky part now is trying to figure out how to create quality content for these accounts and to figure out how our presence on these sites can translate into increased gifts to the annual fund."

After gaining friends/fans/contacts, what kind of maintenance does the site require?

"The only social networking service I've been really excited about is Twitter. So it's the one that I've really put energy into in terms of content and reaching out to fans and followers. I look each follower up in our alumni database — if there's a match I send a hello message, welcoming them to give me suggestions for improvements. There is good potential for growth with this — we could do Tweet-ups or target e-mail messages or any number of different targeted messages or events. The nice thing is there's no fee to have an account on any of these sites and we don't pay someone to create content. Most tweets are auto-generated from official college RSS feeds. Depending on my workload, I may spend zero to three hours a week on maintaining the accounts.

"We are considering implementing personal fundraising sites. They were very successful with the Obama campaign, and I've seen them for friends running marathons. But because the cost to implement them is fairly high, and there is some uncertainty that the success they have in irregular, deadline-oriented fundraising projects will be able to translate to giving annually to an educational institution."

What kind of response has your office seen to their social networking efforts?

"One challenge has been to quantify the response we've had. There's no real way to know if our presence on these sites results

in increased giving.... Our official annual giving Facebook account has 20 fans. The official St. Olaf Alumni Facebook group has about 2,500 members.... An unofficial, renegade and fairly inactive Facebook St. Olaf College fan page has 3,000 fans. By contrast, our MySpace had 37 views in the

> **Check Out Social Network Sites**
> ✓ LinkedIn (www.linkedin.com/groups?=gid= 41543)
> ✓ Myspace (www.myspace.com/ ucsantabarbara)
> ✓ Twitter (www.twitter.com/macalester)

past year. Then, our alumni LinkedIn group has 2,250 members. Our Twitter has 500 followers (20 to 30 of whom are traceable alumni) and each tweet link gets four to 35 clicks.

"In terms of Facebook fundraising, an attempt to raise money via Facebook cause bore only $35 in revenue. But when comparing fiscal year '08 to fiscal year '09, we saw a 60 percent increase in the number of online gifts and a 38 percent increase in amount raised through our gift site. Our social networking presence could have contributed to this, but if I were to guess, I'd say that it's more of a national trend than a result of our hard e-work."

What are your other fundraising efforts and their relative success? Which are innovative or new for St. Olaf? How are social networking efforts similar or dissimilar to these?

"Within annual giving, our primary programs are volunteer (reunion and non-reunion), direct mail, e-mail, phoning and the Senior Class Campaign.... Our primary work has been to shift focus from institutional fundraising (solicitation that comes from the college: direct mail, e-mail) to peer-to-peer volunteer fundraising (classmate-to-classmate e-mail, phone calls, letters, etc). We've seen great success with this in a handful of classes, and are working to replicate their success across all graduated classes. Social networking sites may eventually help with this, but we have yet to figure out exactly how."

Source: Matthew Fedde, Associate Director of Annual Giving, St. Olaf College, Northfield, MN. Phone (800) 733-6523 or (507) 786-3705.

RAISE MORE ANNUAL GIFTS VIA YOUR WEBSITE, E-MAIL

Give Online Donors Choices

A decision by university relations staff to create an online giving form resulted in a convenient giving tool for donors to Gonzaga University (Spokane, WA).

Dori Sonntag, director of annual giving, says her office, as well as fellow higher education institutions, have witnessed a trend away from other giving methods toward more online giving.

"We realized that we are an Internet society and in order to provide our donors with the best variety of options, we would have to get on board," Sonntag says about expanding the online giving options available to donors.

The form (www.applyweb.com/public/contribute?gonzagac) begins with the donor entering a donation amount (a $20 minimum; see graphic, below). Donors then designate if they wish to apply the full amount to a single fund or multiple funds. Donors reenter the amount and select a department/category from a drop-down menu.

Sonntag says these categories are updated annually according to the university's need. Some examples include: 2008 annual campaign, senior fund, performing arts, athletics, technology, residence hall renovations, mission-justice, etc.

Once a giving category is selected, another drop-down menu is available to select a specific fund applicable to that department/ category (e.g., for the 2008 annual campaign donors can select from three choices: scholarships, College of Arts and Sciences; and Great

Teachers Program).

Donors then select if the gift is a one-time contribution or a recurring donation (allowing the donor to select from monthly payments indefinitely, for 'x' amount of months or quarterly).

Through the online form, donors also can:

- Designate if they would like to be recognized for their gift or remain anonymous.

- Update their spouse and children information.

- Choose if their or their spouse's company will match their gift.

Online donors are asked to identify how they found the site (e.g., referred by a solicitation letter; student Telefund caller; university employee [with menu to select employee's name]; pledge reminder; e-mail communication; browsing the Web; or other).

Sonntag says during the 2006-2007 fiscal year (ending in May 2007), 355 donors contributed $105,000 through the online giving form. That was a 20 percent increase over the previous year. This year gifts through January 2008 have already surpassed last year's totals, with 243 donors giving $110,000.

Source: Dori Sonntag, Director of Annual Giving, Gonzaga University, Spokane, WA. Phone (509) 323-6149. E-mail: Sonntag@gonzaga.edu

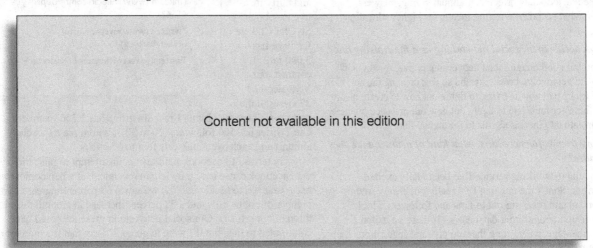

Content not available in this edition

Mention Online Giving On All Pledge Forms

Content not available in this edition

Do all of your pledge forms invite donors to make online contributions? It's wise to include that option since it might be perceived by some as being easier than writing a check and mailing it. Plus, online gifts save you postage.

Also, if your online giving program makes it possible, consider instructing donors to fill in a particular coupon code that allows them to receive a special premium as a thank-you for their generosity. By doing this, you can track the gift to a particular direct mail effort to measure its response rate.

RAISE MORE ANNUAL GIFTS VIA YOUR WEBSITE, E-MAIL

What to Include On Your Online Donation Form

Creating an online donation form? Don't forget to include the following items:

- Fields for first and last name, street, city, state, ZIP, country, phone, e-mail.

- A statement that indicates what the donor would like to do: "I would like to donate to XYZ Organization..."

- Giving levels and the ability to check the level at which they wish to give and a field to specify a dollar amount.

- A statement that you are a 501(c)(3) organization and that all contributions are tax-deductible.

- A statement about site security.

- Fields for cardholder information and a place to indicate if it is same as donor information.

- Types of credit cards you accept and fields for card number, expiration date and security code (and what that is).

- Reset and Submit buttons, plus a Review button to check information.

- A list of other ways to donate (phone, mail, in person, etc.).

- A list of specific projects to fund.

- Alternative contact information in case the form doesn't work or donor wishes to give through other means.

Fund Operational Expenses

Everyone knows nonprofits need to pay the electric bill, but few people want their gifts used for such a mundane purpose.

So how do you sell the need for operational, administrative and fundraising expenses? Add a line to donor pledge forms.

Donors to Texas Christian University (Fort Worth, TX) can designate online gifts to one of 16 programs or expenses, but the default selection is The University's greatest need.

Adding a similar line to your pledge form will allow donors to put their trust in you and give you flexibility with their gift.

Source: Carrie Moore, Assistant Director, Donor Relations, Texas Christian University, Fort Worth, TX. Phone (817) 257-6965. E-mail: cmoore2@tcu.edu

---

Online Fundraising Tip

- Do you ever see a feature on some other nonprofit's Web site that you want to copy but forget to do? To prevent that from happening, start a list of particular features you find on other Web sites that you want to implement one day. Then you'll be prepared to make those updates at the appropriate time.

- Pay attention to timing — Time e-mail appeals to immediately follow big news (about your organization or news that coincides with your organization's work) that has caught the public's attention.

Link Blog Posts to Giving Page

Keep people up to speed on your organization and its cause and boost fundraising efforts through a Web log or blog.

A blog "is a cost-effective way to stay in touch with supporters, spread our mission and beef up our online presence," says Robin Donovan, communications and outreach, Center for Respite Care (Cincinnati, OH).

"A blog is one tool nonprofits can use to keep supporters connected," Donovan says. "Supporters who feel that the day-to-day life of the organization is open to them are more likely to give. Plus, it is one more way to keep first-time volunteers, donors and friends engaged after their initial contact with us."

Blogs provide the perfect opportunity to promote special events, solicit in-kind donations, network and discuss issues important to your organization.

For example, a recent blog entry by Donovan explaining the need for helping the homeless in the winter included a direct link to the organization's online fundraising page.

Michael Foxworth, executive director, The Foothills Foundation/Foothill Presbyterian Hospital (Glendora, CA), also uses a blog as a key communications tool.

"Because the blog is, by nature, much more dynamic than the website and does not require extensive programming or HTML knowledge, nontechnical contributors can easily manage and post information to the blog," Foxworth says.

"There are many valuable blog hosting sites available for the beginner," he says. "Try it. If you can e-mail, you can blog."

Before you begin, Donovan recommends doing your research and being prepared to discuss the need of a blog. Additionally, she says, "learn to write in a style that works online and polish your writing to avoid excessive length. Post regularly, include photos and read related posts as much as you can. Also, read blogs about non-profit blogging and communications."

Sources: Robin Donovan, Communications and Outreach, Center for Respite Care, Cincinnati, OH. Phone (513) 621-1868. E-mail: respitesupport@zoomtown.com. Blog: http://centerforrespitecare.wordpress.com Michael Foxworth, Executive Director, The Foothill Foundation/Foothill Presbyterian Hospital, Glendora, CA. Phone (626) 857-3349. E-mail: mfoxworth@mail.cvhp.org. Blog: www.foothillfoundation.blogspot.com

RAISE MORE ANNUAL GIFTS VIA YOUR WEBSITE, E-MAIL

Firsthand Advice for Creating User-friendly Online Wish List

Could your organization benefit from an online wish list?

Officials with the Mountain View Branch, Anchorage Public Library (Anchorage, AK), realized such a project could offer a unique opportunity to help fill new bookshelves added in the branch's expansion project.

Linda Klein, youth services librarian, says since launching the wish list in November 2007, some 80 items have been purchased for the youth literature section.

"Donors responded to the wish list project immediately," says Klein. "During a fundraising event for the branch, we set up a laptop and unveiled the Amazon wish list page (www.amazon.com/gp/registry/wishlist/K73U9TAJQ707/ref=cm_wl_rlist_go). We had a few donors make purchases that very night."

Klein answers a few questions about the wish list program:

"What is an online wish list program?"

"Much like a bridal registry, online wish lists allow you to identify a specific set of items that your organization needs. The needed items are posted on the seller's website as a wish list allowing donors to purchase the specified items from the list. The items are then sent directly to the organization from the seller."

"Why did your organization decide to implement such a program?"

"This wish list project was created to benefit one of our library branches that was closed in May 2007 and will be reopened sometime this year. Because the branch will be greatly expanded when reopened, and its collection is in need of many new materials, we decided to use an online program that would make it easy for people to support the library in a concrete way."

"How does the program work?"

"We set up a nonprofit account with Amazon (www.amazon.com) that is accessed with a user name and password so we can control the content of the wish list. The program allows us to place a description about the wish list and how it would serve our library on the Amazon site.

"I had compiled a list of books, primarily children's and young adult literature, since that is the area with the greatest need because of the expansion at the library branch. I search through Amazon's site for the titles, and with little more than a click of a button I added them to the wish list. As items were purchased, I replenished the wish list with different titles from my original list.

"For library patrons, it's easy to make a gift. They can find a link to the Amazon wish list from our Web page. From there, they can see the items we've identified that we need, how much it costs, and whether or not it has already been purchased by someone else."

"How do you recognize the donors who make purchases from the wish list?"

"We place a label inside each book explaining that the item was purchased through the generous support of our wish list by library patrons."

"How does the library promote the wish list?"

"There is a link on our main website which goes to a page that explains the functions of the wish list. That page has a link directly to the Amazon wish list. We have also promoted the program using bookmarks that are available at every branch and through a link on the branch's Web page."

"What advice would you offer other nonprofits interested in creating an online wish list?"

"Go with a reputable company that has experience with online wish lists. Amazon has been used by other libraries for this kind of function, so we felt confident that we could benefit from their experience. Identify a specific need or target group you are trying to benefit rather than scattershot trying to solve all your problems with a wish list. It is easier to manage and promote a list that has a specific focus."

Source: Linda Klein, Youth Services Librarian, Muldoon Branch, Anchorage Public Library, Anchorage, AK. Phone (907) 343-4032. E-mail: kleinlm@muni.org

Steps to Create Your Online Wish List

If your organization is interested in pursuing an online wish list program, Linda Klein, youth services librarian, Anchorage Public Library (Anchorage, AK), recommends these steps:

1. **Identify the need you are trying to fill.** "We knew from studying the neighborhood that this library would serve a large immigrant population and many families with small children," says Klein. The branch was also aware of its gap in the collection.

2. **Develop a master list.** To populate the wish list, Klein created a master list of every book she thought the library should have for the juvenile and young adult sections. "I used resources such as award-winner lists, websites with recommended books and publications (books and magazines) to identify the must-haves for any juvenile collection," she says.

3. **Involve interested parties in your wish list.** "Decide who in your organization will have access to the account and share the login information with those people," she says. "We formed a small impromptu committee of our collection development specialist and our technical services librarian and others to iron out the details (e.g., what materials to include or not, whether to acknowledge individual donors, and how to word the blurb on Amazon's site and our website)."

4. **Set up your account.**

5. **Populate the wish list.** By using your master list and matching your needs with what is available at the bookseller's site, create your online wish list. Keep track on your master list what has been added to the list, items purchased and new titles for purchase.

RAISE MORE ANNUAL GIFTS VIA YOUR WEBSITE, E-MAIL

Boost End-of-the-year Giving With Online Wish List

Wish lists are tried-and-true ways to generate targeted support.

If you already have an online wish list, add some attention-getting items and get the word out about year-end opportunities through print and electronic communications.

**Wish Lists May Be Basic Laundry Lists
Or Highly Detailed Documents**

Some organizations' wish lists include a simple checklist of needs (e.g., copy paper, postage stamps). Others go on to include a price estimate and brief description. Still others design highly detailed wish lists complete with photos, how the items will specifically benefit the nonprofit's mission and more.

The Berrien County Council for Children/The Children's Assessment Center (St. Joseph, MI) has a two-part wish list accessible by a direct link on its website's navigation bar (http://berrienchild.org/wish_list.html).

In addition to expected, less expensive wish-list items, such as printer cartridges and cleaning supplies, the nonprofit lists more creative ways to help, such as purchasing or partially funding an internal voicemail system ($3,000) or sponsoring brochure printing costs ($2,000).

Tia Miller, executive director, says since creating the online wish list in 2007, they have received a number of items, including office desks and children's supplies. She recommends being as specific as possible and including a price estimate to help guarantee you receive exactly what you need.

Another organization finding success with an online wish list is the Animal Medical Center (New York, NY). The wish list (shown in part at right) has brought in about $12,000 worth of gifts and goods in its first year, says Brandi Perrow, associate director of development.

The organization's wish list includes a photo, reason item is needed, cost and, if applicable, the amount raised toward the purchase of that item.

For example, a picture of a severely obese dog accompanies this text: "Fitness Maintenance for Fido. Some of our animal friends carry a little too much around the waist. Help the AMC obtain weight scales to monitor and manage obesity and diabetes. Needs: 1. Price Each: $1,200 ($300 raised)."

**Offer Wished-for Items
From Small to Large Price Ranges**

When offering a wish list, Perrow says it is important to include items of varying costs to appeal to donors from all financial backgrounds.

What is the appeal of a wish list? "I think donors feel more connected when they can buy something on your list. They are fulfilling one of your wishes," Perrow says. Additionally, "Donors are getting very savvy, and they are concerned with where their money goes.... There is a comfort level with knowing exactly where their money is going and how it is being used."

Sources: Tia Miller, Executive Director, Berrien County Council for Children/The Children's Assessment Center, St. Joseph, MI. Phone (269) 556-9640.
E-mail: tmiller@berrienchild.org
Brandi Perrow, Associate Director of Development, The Animal Medical Center, New York, NY. Phone (212) 329-8662.
E-mail: brandi.perrow@amcny.org. Website: www.amcny.org

Content not available in this edition

Online Giving Tip

- To bring back visitors to your website repeatedly (and hopefully encourage multiple gifts), vary your site's content with fresh news and photos. A content management system (CMS) allows non-programmers to regularly upload new text and photos.

RAISE MORE ANNUAL GIFTS VIA YOUR WEBSITE, E-MAIL

Mini-websites Help Raise Funds for Nonprofit's Mission

If your organization's membership and fundraising staff are stretched thin or you are simply looking for a way to engage members, consider sharing important duties with your supporters by creating a program that lets them take an active role in raising funds for your mission.

After years of donor-led fundraising events (e.g., birthday parties, weddings, special events, etc.) staff with the World Wildlife Fund (WWF) of Washington, DC, decided a change was needed, and launched Panda Pages in summer 2008.

Panda Pages is a section on WWF's website where persons create their own mini-websites to help raise money, raise awareness for the organization or a particular issue and connect with family and friends.

"The process of the fundraising events was cumbersome for donors and time-intensive for staff to manage," says David Glass, director, online marketing. "Our donors had to do much of the outreach, communication, fundraising and operations on their own. And, the entire effort was off-line, which made it challenging for a donor to gather and consolidate donations.

"It was time to give the donor much more control by putting the fundraising tools into the hands of our energetic and passionate supporters," he says.

Now by visiting the Panda Pages section (www.worldwildlife.org/mypanda) on WWF's website, supporters can customize a page in support of the organization's mission in about 10 minutes. The page can be customized to mark a special occasion, honor a friend or loved one, or simply highlight their passion for protecting endangered species.

The mini-websites allow supporters to:

✓ Send e-mails to friends asking them to visit the page.
✓ Raise money to help support WWF's conservation work.
✓ Connect with members who are passionate about conservation.
✓ Upload and share photos of favorite animals and nature places.
✓ Help protect endangered species and places around the world.

Around 1,000 pages have been created since the first launch..

Glass says supporters have two options when creating a page: public and private. A public page can be viewed or used by anyone who comes across the site, while only those who are specially invited may see a private page. Glass says near the holidays many families use the private pages to share information related to conservation and wildlife, conduct private fundraising, and share gift giving and donations online.

Source: David Glass, Director, Online Marketing, World Wildlife Fund, Washington, DC. Phone (202) 293-4800. E-mail: David.glass@wwfus.org

---

Factors to Consider With User-based Fundraising Tool

A user-based fundraising tool like Panda Pages has several appealing benefits, says David Glass, director, online marketing, World Wildlife Fund (Washington, DC).

Those benefits include:

1. Donors and friends get a convenient, easy-to-use and efficient way to support their favorite cause.
2. The nonprofit gets an economical and efficient way to connect with many donors at a time for event-, theme- or topic-based fundraising.

Glass also shares two issues that are important to acknowledge with a new tool like this:

1. Putting more control in the hands of your organization's friends and donors means expecting and accepting that the messaging and language they use will vary and most likely be as on-message as the language used by the organization to promote its own issues.
2. It's useful to build in training and awareness with a customer service team to help with any questions or concerns a donor may have.

Online Pledge Event Tools Improve Fundraising Results

How can you make the most of pledge events?

An online team fundraising system helps boost the success of the Walk for Hunger for Project Bread (East Boston, MA), says Margaret Sloat, event director. The 2008 Walk for Hunger brought in $3.8 million from more than 40,000 walkers, despite rain on the day of the event.

Prior to adding the online system, Sloat says, walkers struggled with asking for pledges from people living outside their local area. Online fundraising enables them to ask family and friends who live far away to help, boosting the potential donor pool.

"A student in Cambridge can expand their donor pool to include aunts in California and a grandmother in Florida," says Sloat. "These donors can respond to an e-mail sent to them by their niece by clicking to our donation form and making their donation online — saving time, postage and hassle for both the walker and the donor."

Project Bread's staff also uses e-mail to send fundraising tips to walkers, which Sloat says they find very helpful: "For those of us in the fundraising profession, it might be intuitive: first you have to figure out who to ask, and you have to figure out what to ask them for, etc.," she says. "But when we're reaching out to 40,000 people who don't do fundraising on a regular basis, it seems very intimidating."

The weekly e-mails break the process of gathering pledges into small, manageable steps covering all the traditional steps in the fundraising process. For example, a message may suggest walkers take 10 minutes to write a statement about why they're participating in the Walk for Hunger, or remind them to thank their donors.

Finally, the Walk for Hunger's online system keeps staff informed of each walker's progress. "We used to not know how much people were going to raise or who was participating until we got the data post-walk, but now we know how many people have registered and we know what their fundraising goals are," Sloat says. Knowing this, staff can encourage the walkers as they collect pledges, and immediately congratulate them if they raise the $500 needed to put them in the honorary Heart and Sole Circle.

Sloat says the feedback often spurs walkers to work even harder: "They say, 'You know, I could do a little bit more.'"

However, Sloat emphasizes that organizations shouldn't interact with participants solely online: "We still do mailings and rounds of phone calls to our top supporters, and don't rely only on e-mail and our website to continue to build relationships with them."

Source: Margaret Sloat, Director of the Walk for Hunger, Project Bread, East Boston, MA. Phone (617) 239-2525. E-mail: margaret_sloat@projectbread.org

RAISE MORE ANNUAL GIFTS VIA YOUR WEBSITE, E-MAIL

Organization Turns Supporters Into Fundraisers

What are you doing to move faithful supporters to becoming fundraisers for your cause?

At the Austin Children's Shelter (ACS) of Austin, TX, staff invites supporters to create their own online fundraising page.

"The Austin Children's Shelter Tributes tool provides individuals the opportunity to support the shelter in a unique way and share their personal story, honor a friend or loved one on their birthday, anniversary or special occasion, or honor the memory of a friend or loved one who has passed," says Steve Anderson, director of development. "Each page tells the story of a special person and provides the opportunity to make an online donation to the Austin Children's Shelter.... Individual fundraising pages really give donors and prospective donors another avenue to help raise awareness and funds for ACS."

In the first six months of offering this feature, supporters have created 15 pages and raised approximately $8,000, Anderson says.

ACS contracts with Convio, Inc. (Austin, TX) to provide the feature for a fee. The shelter's marketing director approves the individual pages, and ACS staff promote the feature through links on its home page, in its quarterly newsletter and in appeals.

To create a tribute page, supporters:

✓ Access the tributes page from the ACS website.
✓ Create the page by completing basic information, including personal information, fund name and fund goal and, if they choose, adding a personal story and photo.
✓ Share the completed fundraising page with friends and family via e-mail, encouraging them to visit the page and submit an online donation.

Source: Steve Anderson, Director of Development, Austin Children's Shelter, Austin, TX. Phone (512) 499-0090.
E-mail: andersons@austinchildrenshelter.org

Donor-centric Catalog Lets Prospects Browse Giving Choices

Are you looking for a one-stop resource for donors and development staff alike? Consider the giving catalog produced by the University of Pittsburgh (Pittsburgh, PA).

Jasmine Hoffman, manager of public relations in institutional advancement, says that since its inception in December 2008, the online catalog has received more than 1,200 unique page views and is the seventh most-visited page on the site.

Hoffman says the most interesting analysis though is in the page's bounce rate.

"The bounce rate measures the number of people who leave the site after viewing only one page," she says. "Eighty-seven percent of the users who visit the giving catalog are navigating through multiple pages in the catalog. The giving catalog is providing prospective donors with quality information about giving while they research their philanthropic interests."

So how does the giving catalog work?

Prospective donors visit the website at www.giveto.pitt.edu/catalog/index.asp through an easy link on the home page of the university's website. There they are able to research giving opportunities through four filters: university priorities, dollar amount, key words and build your own gift. Once they have reviewed their options, they can be linked directly to a development officer. Inquiries go directly to the development officer who is fundraising for that particular initiative.

The site also allows development staff to quickly send information to prospective donors. "For instance, if a donor wants more information about a Student Resources Fund in the School of Arts and Sciences, the development officer can quickly e-mail an information sheet about that gift to a donor," says Hoffman.

Hoffman says their primary goal in developing the catalog was to serve as an information source for donors and development officers. "It's doing that and more. Feedback so far has been positive, with users finding the catalog intuitive and easy to use."

Source: Jasmine Hoffman, Manager of Public Relations in Institutional Advancement, University of Pittsburgh, Pittsburgh, PA. Phone (412) 624-5847.
E-mail: jasmine.hoffman@ia.pitt.edu

Three Tools to Evaluate Giving Catalogs

Jasmine Hoffman, manager of public relations in institutional advancement, University of Pittsburgh (Pittsburgh, PA) says their online giving catalog has been a hit with alumni, prospective donors and development officers alike. How did they know that would be the case when they were developing the catalog? They did thorough research and utilize Web analytics. Hoffman offers the following tips to make sure similar tools work effectively for you:

1. **Do your research first.** Hoffman says focus groups and online surveys told them that many of their donors visit the university's website to explore giving opportunities before completing an online gift or contacting the development office. This led them to believe the catalog would be a natural extension of that need for research and information.

2. **Understand how your donors think.** A comprehensive card sort analysis helped them understand how donors organize giving opportunities and terms on the website. Hoffman says, "The card sort analysis helped us identify the categories and terminology to use in the giving catalog. We wanted the giving catalog to be donor-centric so we thought it was appropriate to organize it according to the responses from the card sort analysis."

3. **Use the technology available.** Hoffman says Web analytics have allowed them to see that the students' category is the most successful area within the giving catalog and that most Web visitors are navigating to that section of the catalog first. Analytics have also allowed them to know how many unique page views the site has received and how many people leave the website after viewing only one page. All of this information allows them to tweak the catalog to make it more user friendly.

63

MEMORIAL, IN-TRIBUTE GIFTS OFFER ADDED WAYS TO RAISE FUNDS

Although memorial and in-tribute giving might be more appropriate for some types of nonprofits that others, this method of building support should not be overlooked and underestimated. Some organizations have had significant success in broadening their base of donors by focusing more on memorial and in-tribute gift marketing. For other organizations, what began a relationship with a small memorial gift was nurtured into a long-term friendship that resulted in major gifts, both outright and planned.

Point Out Recent Memorials and Their Uses

Memorial gifts help honor the memory of loved ones and friends, they build loyalty to the recipient charity and they can help broaden a charity's base of support.

If your organization deserves to be the recipient of more memorial gifts, show the public how much you treasure them:

✓ Include a list of all memorials (and those who gave to them) in your annual honor roll of contributors.

✓ Mention recent memorials in each issue of the newsletter or magazine you distribute to your mailing list.

✓ Personally thank everyone who makes a memorial contribution

and inform the family of those who contributed and how much.

✓ Whenever a memorial of any size is established, send an update to all contributors telling them how the funds were (or will be) used.

✓ Do a feature story on some of the memorial gifts you have received in the past and how those gifts impact those you serve.

✓ Create a recognition wall or walkway or some other lasting tribute to anyone who has been memorialized at your charity.

✓ Hold a yearly memorial service inviting the family and friends of those who have been memorialized in the past.

Be Prepared to Explore Named Memorials

Don't underestimate the importance of exploring major gift opportunities — or at least planting the seed — during the loss of a loved one.

It goes without saying that it's important to use a great deal of tact in determining if and when you should broach the subject of a memorial with the deceased's loved ones. However, it is very appropriate to at least outline the options available when family members come to you or publicly announce that memorial gifts may be directed to your charity. When that does occur, follow these guidelines:

1. **Cover procedures for handling memorial gifts as soon as you are notified.** Explain that all memorial gifts directed to your charity will be placed in a holding account until a later date when you and the appropriate family members can meet to determine how the gifts will be used. Also inform the family that, in addition to sending donors a note of thanks, the names, addresses and gift amounts, you will give the names of all the contributors to the family.

2. **Be sure your charity is well represented at the funeral and/or wake.** If your charity has been or might be named a recipient of memorial gifts, it's only appropriate that your presence is obvious. You might

even want to provide flowers or a plant.

3. **Follow up within days.** Depending on the circumstances and the wishes of family members, set an appointment to meet and review memorial possibilities. Have a standard presentation developed — such as the example below — to outline gift possibilities.

Sample memorial presentation to use with family members of the deceased.

Memorial Gift Options

<u>If memorial gifts amount to less than $1,000</u>
Have a prepared wish list of needs — perhaps identified by your development committee — with attached dollar amounts. Include a range of dollar amounts and uses. This allows families to decide on the exact use of memorial funds without simply having funds disappear into your organization's annual budget.

Explain that the memorial — plus the names of all who contributed — will be listed in your organization's annual report of contributors.

<u>For memorial gifts between $1,000 and $10,000</u>
Once again, share a wish list of needs, only this time identify more significant needs that include naming opportunities based on the overall amount contributed toward the memorial. Memorial gifts totaling $2,000, for instance, could be used to name an item — a flowing water fountain or a meeting room table — while a gift of $9,000 might name an office or a particular room in honor of someone.

<u>For memorial gifts that may amount to $10,000 or more</u>
Gifts totaling $10,000 or more — even if given by family members over a period of years (or through a bequest) — could be used to establish various types of named endowment funds or to name even more significant physical projects (e.g., The Ben Michner Cancer Center, The Mark Steffenson Reading Room). Once again, it's helpful to have an identified list of needs. With this level of giving, however, it's important that the donor have some say in shaping the exact use of the gift so he/she develops a greater sense of ownership.

MEMORIAL, IN-TRIBUTE GIFTS OFFER ADDED WAYS TO RAISE FUNDS

Turn One-time Memorial Contributors Into Annual Ones

A well-known, highly respected board member dies. The obituary states that all memorial gifts be directed to your charity. For the next several days, you receive an outpouring of checks from those who knew and respected the board member. Many memorial gifts are from first-time contributors — 61 gifts from first-time contributors to be exact.

Now that you have 61 new first-time contributors, what do you plan to do to encourage repeat giving? How can you begin to build loyalty among this group? Any or all of these suggestions will help:

Acknowledge with tact, professionalism. Send a personal note of thanks indicating you will notify the deceased's family immediately of their act of kindness. (You might even copy your notification to the contributor.)

Recognize. Explain that the contributor's name will appear in your honor roll of contributors (whenever it is published) as a memorial gift. Ask how the name should appear when you send your gift acknowledgment letter.

Extend a welcome. Send another letter and welcome packet within weeks of the memorial gift, one that opens your door to the contributor and invites him/her to become of member of your organizational family. Include your most recent newsletter and literature that helps the contributor appreciate the worthiness of continued association with your organization.

Consider involving the family of the deceased in cultivating these first-time contributors. Their level of involvement can be minimal or extensive depending on their interest and state of mind.

Make a personal call on these first-time contributors. Whether its accomplished on your own, with the aid of someone else or you assign the call to another staff member, there's nothing like a personal call to say "you're important to us."

Pending Option Gives Grieving Donors Time

When a loved one dies, families can become overwhelmed with all of the arrangements, decisions and grief.

Bonny Kellermann, director of memorial gifts, MIT (Cambridge, MA), says giving families time to consider all of their options ensures a meaningful gift to the school.

"Very often, when a family has lost a loved one, they are not ready to decide the details of how to memorialize them," Kellermann says. "Allowing a cushion of time to make this decision is greatly appreciated by the families."

MIT allows families to establish funds with a purpose to be determined later through their pending memorial gift accounts. The decision of what to use the funds for can be deferred for up to two years. When the account is established, families are informed that any funds not designated within two years will be used for unrestricted purposes.

The pending option gives families time to think about an appropriate, meaningful memorial and allows time for them to receive memorial gifts from other people, which can be a factor in determining how the fund will be used.

Donors also benefit emotionally from the pending option.

"Many families really appreciate the fact that they can postpone this decision to a time after they have grieved or dealt with estate issues," says Kellermann. "The donor benefits by not being forced to make a decision at a time that is very stressful."

"Often, when a family has lost a loved one, they are not ready to decide the details of how to memorialize them. Allowing a cushion of time to make this decision is greatly appreciated."

As a result, MIT also benefits. "Since the donors have the opportunity to take time to consider what is really important to them," Kellerman says, "they may be inclined to give more than they might have otherwise given."

Source: Bonny Kellermann, Director of Memorial Gifts, MIT, Cambridge, MA. Phone (617) 253-9722. E-mail: bonnyk@MIT.EDU

Memorial Fund Options Help Focus Donor Intent

When Nancy Cushing-Daniels — beloved Spanish professor at Gettysburg College (Gettysburg, PA) — passed away in June 2009, her family approached college officials with an idea for a memorial fund. Their idea: to honor Cushing-Daniels' memory and passion for both learning languages and embracing cultures around the world.

If only it was always so easy to determine and honor donor intent.

It can be, if you have options, says Ashlyn Sowell, interim vice president for development, alumni and parent relations.

"We try to be prepared (for inquiries into memorial options) by having options," says Sowell. "For example, we have some benches and trees on campus that we designate for families who want a physical memorial. For other folks, we discuss funds like Professor Cushing-Daniels', which is more specific and restricted."

Sowell says college officials do not do a great deal of active fundraising for memorial gifts, letting the families drive that for the most part. What is most important, says Sowell, is being patient and understanding. "Memorial funds take time," she says, "and there are many emotions involved."

Source: Ashlyn Sowell, Interim Vice President for Development, Alumni and Parent Relations, Gettysburg College, Gettysburg, PA. Phone (717) 337-6503. E-mail: asowell@gettysburg.edu

MEMORIAL, IN-TRIBUTE GIFTS OFFER ADDED WAYS TO RAISE FUNDS

Encourage Birthday and Anniversary Tribute Gifts

Many nonprofits have programs encouraging those on their mailing lists to honor friends' and families' birthdays and/or anniversaries with a contribution.

If that makes sense for your organization, here are some of the procedure's key components:

1. Publicize your in-tribute program, and make it easy for persons to make a gift. Mention the program in your newsletter; conduct a mailing to everyone on your list that explains the program and includes some forms and return envelopes they can use to send in in-honor gifts.

2. Include a list of persons who have been honored in each issue

of your newsletter, listing the honoree first and then the person who made the in-tribute gift.

3. Whenever an in-honor gift is received, send a personalized note to the honoree informing him/her that a gift was made and who made the gift.

4. Consider getting a sponsor to underwrite the cost of supplying each honoree with an inexpensive gift (i.e., free yogurt coupon or a movie pass) from your organization that can accompany your notification note. The gesture allows you to also express congratulations to the honoree at no cost to your organization.

Memorial to Young Leader Inspires Emerging Leaders

The founding members of the Skip Cline Young Leadership Society of Morton Plant Mease Foundation (Clearwater, FL) recognized a desire of younger adults in the community to become more involved with their hospitals. They also recognized a natural connection in naming the society after their friend, Harry Sykes "Skip" Cline, Jr., who died an untimely death.

To the society's founders, "Skip embodied the ideals of a young leader," says Eric Barsema, community impact manager. "Skip was also raised in a family which contributed time, treasure and talent to our community and to Morton Plant Hospital.... They thought the group could build on his family's tradition of community involvement and philanthropy."

The society has raised more than $360,000 since being founded in 2004.

Members, aged 21 to 45, commit to make gifts of at least $500 annually. Members also commit to becoming better informed and more involved with their hospitals through a variety of social and educational events, including happy hours, fundraising events and educational lectures, as well as opportunities to mingle with physicians and hospital leadership. Generally, there is some type of event

for members every month.

Donations are typically unrestricted, going to the hospital's area of greatest need. Barsema says the society is leaning toward designating gifts to specific projects in the hospital, a request the foundation is more than happy to accommodate.

With approximately 250 members, the group's size does pose a bit of a challenge, Barsema says: "Many of the founding members were in their late 30s when they launched the society, and now, five years later, are asking to be able to stay a part of the group after they turn 46."

The society's retention rate of more than 90 percent speaks to Barsema's unique dilemma, though he admits it's not a bad one to have. "Of all the foundation's annual giving societies," he says, "Skip Cline members seem to have the greatest camaraderie and pride for their philanthropic support of the hospitals of Morton Plant Mease."

Source: Eric Barsema, Community Impact Manager, Morton Plant Mease Foundation, Clearwater, FL. Phone (727) 462-7036.
E-mail: mpmfoundation@baycare.org

Leave No Questions Unanswered in Memorial Donors' Minds

What gift acknowledgment procedures do you follow when someone makes a memorial gift to your charity?

In addition to informing the family of the deceased of memorial gifts — who gave, when and how much — be sure to inform the contributor that the family of the deceased will be notified of the gift.

The example at right helps clarify the charity's intent to inform the family of the deceased.

Dear <Name>:

We want to take this opportunity to thank you for your recent gift in memory of <name of deceased>. We know <name of deceased>'s family will want to know of your thoughtful gesture, so we will inform them within the next few days.

In addition, when our 2005 Annual Honor Roll of Contributors is distributed in <month>, your name will appear as a memorial contributor under the name of <name of deceased>.

Follow Up With Those Who Make Memorial Gifts

What sorts of follow-up do you take with those who make memorial (even in tribute) gifts to your nonprofit? They obviously receive some sort of thank-you from your organization, but what else occurs?

Whenever you receive a sufficient number and/or amount of memorial gifts to do something significant — start a scholarship, purchase a major piece of equipment or renovate or refurbish a room — everyone who helped make that project possible should be

updated on its progress and included in celebrating its completion.

Those follow-up actions may include: a tour or demonstration, receiving a photo of the completed project, being invited to an unveiling or dedication, having their names listed in your honor roll of contributors and more.

As memorial donors witness your thoughtful acts of stewardship, they will become more likely to remember your organization in other ways as well.

MEMORIAL, IN-TRIBUTE GIFTS OFFER ADDED WAYS TO RAISE FUNDS

Tribute Program Recognizes Caregivers, Raises $1 Million

Putting a creative twist on tribute gifts, a California healthcare system has raised more than $1 million in less than four years.

Through the Guardian Angel Tribute Program for Sharp HealthCare (San Diego, CA), a patient can honor a special caregiver by making a donation in his or her name. There is no minimum donation, and patients can honor individuals or entire departments.

"This is a way for our patients to recognize any of their caregivers — a nurse, a physician, a housekeeper — who has done something wonderful for them," says Christina Jordan, senior development officer.

Here's how the tribute program works:

- Patients in a Sharp HealthCare's hospital receive a bookmark introducing the tribute program. The bookmark, left when housekeeping staff clean a room, features the program's logo, brief description and place to write special caregivers' names.

- Four to six months after the patient's hospital stay, he or she receives a direct-mail piece that further explains the Guardian Angel program and invites patients to honor a physician, nurse or other caregiver with a donation in his or her name. Additionally, tabletop displays with donation envelopes are at each of the nurses' stations, as well as some offices.

- When gifts arrive, development staff send a thank-you to the donor within 48 hours.

- Anyone named as a guardian angel receives a letter and special lapel pin. For a person's first recognition, the patient relations director presents the letter and takes a photo of the recipient, sharing details of the patient's story when provided. Since it is common for caregivers to receive recognition multiple times (one doctor has 81 pins), those receiving pins two through nine

and 11 or more are simply sent a letter and pin. The 10th recognition earns a gold pin.

- The development staff mails the donor a second thank-you letter with a photo of the caregiver receiving his or her pin. Jordan notes that the picture taken at the initial presentation is used each time that person is honored.

- Early in the calendar year, donors receive a direct mail piece inviting them to submit a second donation in honor of their guardian angel to celebrate National Doctor's Day in March. As a gift for the physicians, the development office compiles a Doctor's Day booklet that lists guardian angels and donors who honored them.

Since implementing the tribute program four years ago, Jordan says, they have given out more than 5,300 pins to 1,577 guardian angels, with gifts in honor of the recipients exceeding $1 million. The average gift is $250 and the largest, $300,000.

Jordan credits the success of the program — which grew out of a similar, smaller-scale program in place at one of the organization's hospitals — to its simplicity and its natural fit with the The Sharp Experience, a system-wide initiative which focuses on making Sharp HealthCare the best place to work, practice medicine and receive care.

"The biggest benefit is connecting and establishing the relationship among the donor, physician and foundation," she says. "It connects those three dots."

Source: Christina Jordan, Senior Development Officer, Sharp HealthCare, San Diego, CA. Phone (858) 499-4811.
E-mail: christina.jordan@sharp.com

Raise Funds While Honoring Long-time Heroes

Do you have a special employee or much-respected board member who is leaving or retiring? Use the departure of this well-known person as an opportunity to celebrate the person's contributions while raising money for the cause he or she holds so dear.

In three years, the Autumn Gala for the Botsford Foundation (Farmington Hills, MI) has grown from a quaint event to an extravagant hospital fundraiser while keeping one goal in mind: remembering and honoring special hospital leaders.

Diane Shane, manager of foundation programs and services, says the event grew from an idea by a physician leader — also a foundation board member — for a gala to raise funds and honor the hospital's medical staff. The foundation got involved because the medical staff committee needed assistance with the program/advertisement book and auction.

The straightforward gala evolved into a way to also honor a medical staff hero when two longtime physicians passed away that year.

"We were raising money in an effort to honor their memory with the naming of the ambulatory surgery suite and the hospital chapel," Shane says of the premiere event in 2006. "The foundation staff decided to ask the medical staff if proceeds from the gala could be used to match the dollars raised for both initiatives."

The result was a $70,000 gift from the medical staff.

In the gala's second year in 2007, organizers recognized one of

the hospital's founding physicians, with foundation members asking for gifts in the founder's honor. Attendance grew by 100 guests and raised $125,000 for the hospital's capital campaign.

The 2008 event incorporated the retirement of hospital CEO, Gerson I. Cooper, after 50 years of service with the hospital.

"We thought about holding an independent event honoring this legacy leader, but felt we couldn't support two high-priced ticket events," says Shane. "So the event became the Botsford Hospital Medical Staff Autumn Gala and Gerson I. Cooper Tribute."

Because of Cooper's contacts on state and national levels, Shane says the committee felt comfortable reaching beyond traditional limits to sell tickets and seek sponsorships. They set ticket prices at $275 per person and sponsorship levels at $5,000 to $50,000.

The event included a video about Cooper's life, as well as speakers talking about his leadership and legacy at the hospital and at local, regional and national levels.

Bringing in $500,000, the 2008 event raised more than double that of the first two years combined. Proceeds benefited the hospital's cancer center, says Shane, who notes attendance has also grown steadily, 275 guests in 2006 to 400 in 2007 to 650 in 2008.

Source: Diane Shane, Manager of Foundation Programs and Services, The Botsford Foundation, Farmington Hills, MI. Phone (248) 442-5046.
E-mail: dshane@botsford.org

MEMORIAL, IN-TRIBUTE GIFTS OFFER ADDED WAYS TO RAISE FUNDS

Host an Annual Memorial Service

If your organization is the type that encourages memorial gifts and you want to draw more attention to that form of giving — and encourage people to add to memorial funds — consider hosting an annual memorial service at your facility.

An annual memorial service might include the following elements:

- ❑ Inviting the family and friends of all who have been memorialized as a result of gifts to your charity.
- ❑ Establishing an ongoing committee or advisory group to oversee changes and improvements to your program.
- ❑ Printing an honor roll of everyone who has been memorialized in your program.
- ❑ Having a permanent display listing the names of those who have been memorialized.
- ❑ Having someone speak about how the legacy of these deceased individuals will live on through the mission and work of your organization.
- ❑ Reading the names of those who have been memorialized during your service.
- ❑ Inviting those in attendance to consider adding to named memorial funds.

Include Tribute, Memorial Gift Options on Pledge Forms

If you would like to increase the number of memorial and/or in-tribute gifts your charity receives each year, be sure all pledge forms include that gift option along with other gift options.

In addition to specifying the name of the individual being honored or memorialized, the donor can instruct the development office to notify appropriate individuals of the gift. Portions of two pledge forms are shown below.

Please Make My Gift a Tribute	Acknowledge My Gift To	My Information
❑ In Honor Of.... ❑ In Memory Of....	Name	Name
Name	Address	Address
Occasion (Optional)	City State ZIP	City State ZIP
Occasion (Optional)	Your gift will be acknowledged in accordance with your instructions, and the gift amount will not be disclosed.	Daytime Phone E-mail Address

Tribute and Memorial Gifts

❑ This gift is in memory of _____
and/or

❑ This gift is in honor of _____

A notification of your tribute or memorial gift will be sent to the individual listed below. The gift amount will not be indicated.

Individual
to receive notification _____

Address _____

City _____ State _____ ZIP _____

HANDOUTS, COLLATERAL MATERIALS HELP SUPPORT YOUR REQUEST

There's no substitute for the human factor when it comes to inviting gift support, but those collateral materials you use to help make a compelling case are important as well. What you say and how you say it — and how it's presented — all matter. Your collateral materials should support your face-to-face request but should also be able to stand on their own. Following are some ideas to help you think and write more creatively as you prepare these supporting materials.

Use New Approaches for Annual Fund Brochures

Developing annual fund literature for a new fiscal year? Looking for new ways to make a compelling case for annual support?

To avoid reproducing the same old thing, choose from among the following approaches as you develop new materials for your new fiscal year:

1. **Incorporate testimonials.** Testimonials (from those served by your organization, board members, staff, donors, community leaders and others) provide a powerful reason for annual contributions.

2. **Tie annual support to long-range plans.** Summarize key elements of your nonprofit's strategic plans. Show how increased annual giving is necessary to expanding future services.

3. **Zero in on your mission.** Focus on the life blood relationship between annual gifts and mission fulfillment.

4. **Provide a menu of annual gift opportunities.** Share specific needs. Offer choices of gift opportunities and ranges.

5. **Demonstrate the accomplishments of last year's annual fund.** Show donors how last year's support made a noticeable difference. Then make the case for this year's effort.

6. **Emphasize the donor's benefits.** Point out how the donor will benefit — directly or indirectly — by giving to your annual giving campaign (e.g., tax deduction, member benefits, etc.).

7. **Concentrate on the human element.** Focus on one individual who has benefited from your services, or do a day in the life of three or four persons served by your nonprofit.

Put Some Creativity Into Annual Gift Brochures

Your organization's annual giving literature plays a role in annual giving success. Yet chances are not even your most dedicated supporters eagerly anticipate reading it.

While trying to be too clever in your brochure concepts may cause potential donors to miss your point, some planning and brainstorming can pave the way to creating an annual campaign that will both attract positive attention and educate your constituency about the importance of their ongoing support.

Consider these ideas as you plan your annual campaign and publications:

✓ **Combine a brochure with a yearlong calendar.** Using a standard folded size such as 8.5-by-5.5-inch to mail in a 9-by-6-inch booklet envelope — or a format to fit a standard No. 10 business envelope — create a calendar that features a different program or service each month. List important dates related to your organization, regular holidays or even anniversaries of milestones in your history. Place detachable pledge cards or reminders in months when you hope to collect pledge installments.

✓ **Integrate nature into the concept and link it to your mission.** Animals, flowers, seasons and weather affect everyone and offer an endless list of creative possibilities for illustrating your services and values. Use illustrations, original photographs, verse or stories related to the time of year and the natural element you choose to make your points. Carry the ideas a step further with paper and ink choices. Use different shades of the same paper and a different ink color in cost-effective layouts that complement the different sections of your piece.

✓ **Use famous historic figures and children to show possibilities for your future.** Your organization has both a history and a future. Children dressed as their favorite famous person may touch people with the concept that every person, and your programs, have bright promise and possibilities ahead.

✓ **Choose a single graphic symbol that has meaning for your organization or theme.** An antique (or very modern) hourglass, decorative key, eagle, strong oak tree, race car or helping hand carry messages and images you can use as artwork for your brochure as well as related items like T-shirts and hats, and as a bridge in copy that connects the symbol with your mission. Think of the primary positive feelings you wish to convey and a visual image that can mentally connect with your audience.

✓ **A visually and verbally entertaining timeline of your immediate and future goals.** Most organizations have a long-range plan reaching beyond the current fund drive. Starting with the present, offer illustrations and text look at your organization's future. Demonstrate how annual support is critical to fulfillment of future plans.

Even if none of these concepts is quite right for you, use them as a springboard to brainstorm with others and think of your own unique approach.

HANDOUTS, COLLATERAL MATERIALS HELP SUPPORT YOUR REQUEST

Illustrate the Power of Annual Gifts

Whether you're writing copy for an annual fund brochure, a direct mail appeal or your website, it's important for would-be contributors to really know that their gifts make a difference. And that's not always easy to do.

You can help donors understand the significance of their gifts by showing them the size of endowment that would be required to fund their gift each year. For example, an annual gift of $1,000, based on an annual endowment return of five percent, would require a $20,000 endowment gift. Make use of an illustration such as the one shown here to help donors realize the significance of their gifts.

Your Annual Gift Is Powerful!

While you may be unable to give a major endowment gift of $20,000 or more at this time, your gift to the Annual Fund is just as powerful. For example, look what your annual gift is worth in endowment funds this fiscal year, based on a 5 percent annual return:

Annual Gift	Endowment Equivalent
$10,000	$200,000
$5,000	$100,000
$2,500	$50,000
$1,000	$20,000
$500	$10,000

Advice for Creative, Cost-effective Brochures

When you sort your own mail, you likely use your visual and tactile senses as much as you use critical thinking skills: bills in one stack, flimsy flyers and advertising in another, and eye-catching designs printed on attractive paper stock with personal mail.

With a little planning and creativity, you can help ensure that brochures sent to prospects will make it to the keepers stack. If your brochures will be used in racks or accompanied by letters, attractive presentation invites the recipient to take a closer look and read the message.

A few basic design tips and printing ideas will help you plan brochures that stand out from other reading materials and save you money as well:

- **Make two colors of ink look like more.** Most commercial printers have two-color presses. This means it costs little more for you to use two ink colors instead of one, because most presses print both colors in a single pass. Extra cost of a second color is usually a press plate and a negative. If you choose ink colors like red and blue, an overlay of the two colors together will create purple, or yellow and blue will make a green. Use of an overlay of the two base colors as an accent can give added dimension to your brochure for very little money.

- **One ink color may be enough.** Even if your brochure budget or your printed quantity is too small to justify commercial printing, you can create a professional appearance with black or one other color on its own. Include screened or reversed areas to highlight visuals or special text. Experiment with your computer's graphics program to see if it includes special effects such as drop shadows behind text boxes or fonts, outlined type for headlines or titles, and curved or shaped text. Print your original copy in black ink, then take it to your copy center to run in one of their standard colors.

- **Have fun with your paper stock.** No matter how many colors of ink you use, you can add color through your paper

---

Breath New Life Into Your Fund Brochure

Do you find yourself reproducing the same type of annual fund brochure year after year, only with minor changes? Is it difficult to think outside the box in creating new marketing publications?

To breathe new life into your annual fund brochure, give any or all of these ideas a try:

- ✓ Contact a dozen or so development shops around the country and offer to do an exchange: "I'll send you our annual fund brochure if you would be kind enough to share yours with us."

- ✓ Approach a local ad agency to see if you could get some pro-bono assistance with new design concepts that are within your print budget parameters.

- ✓ Sponsor a simple contest aimed at those served by your organization — students, patients, youth. Ask them to complete the statement: "What [name of your organization] means to me and why...." Offer prizes to those whose testimonials you use in your publication.

---

stock. Call a representative from one or more of your local paper companies and ask for swatch books of stocks that meet your needs. If your organization orders lots of printing and paper, they may even bring you a cabinet of all of their house sheets. Most brands and types of paper come in a variety of color choices, textures, weights and laser-compatible surfaces. Many office supply stores carry a good selection of papers that can be bought in quantities of 100 to 500 sheets. Examples include parchments, linens and pebble textures.

- **Experiment with simple folding techniques.** While choosing a readily available paper size like 8.5 X 11 or 11 X 14 inches keeps your costs low, you may design your graphics to show when folded at a certain angle, or fold a standard size vertically rather than horizontally. Getting too complicated can be expensive or cause difficulty for your printer, but asking for advice first can avoid most concerns. Your printer can be a valuable source of ideas for easy but unique folds. Even if others have used the same technique, your design, colors and papers will make yours look new.

- **Ask for costs differences between different weights of the same paper stock.** If you have a choice between a 100# text or an 80# cover of the same paper, the latter is likely to be heavier. If a heavier weight is desirable, ask your printer if the stock is heavy enough to require scoring first. The scores (made on the fold) will help heavier papers fold smoothly and evenly. A lighter weight of the stock may not need scoring before passing through the printer's folding machine and save money. You decide where the extra costs are warranted.

Save attractive brochures and use them for design ideas. Visit with your printer or paper house representative to see how you can achieve a similar effect with minimal resources. Keep in mind that the paper you use is your artistic canvas, and a high-quality stock may cost only slightly more than standard fare.

HANDOUTS, COLLATERAL MATERIALS HELP SUPPORT YOUR REQUEST

Maintain Consistency in Annual Fund Brochures

Creating an annual fund brochure year after year can be challenging.

Although it is important to change and update some elements of the brochure to keep it fresh and appealing, Deborah Kirkland, director of development, The Joy School (Houston, TX), says it's just as important to keep some elements the same.

"Consistency is important," Kirkland says. "Every year when our supporters receive the annual fund brochure, they recognize it. It's become like a brand. It is associated or identified with your organization."

To maintain consistency, she keeps these elements of the report the same each year:

- Logo
- Slogan
- Brochure size
- Reply card
- Overall design template (including leaving plenty of white space and incorporating the school's logo as a bullet point)

To update the publication year to year, she changes the text and photos. Doing so, she says, "shows growth and relevance among issues and topics. It is not static. It shows that we stay current. It makes it present day."

Kirkland, who has been designing annual fund brochures for 10 years, says she works on the project throughout the year. "It's such a creative process," she says. "You cannot sit there and make it happen. Ideas can come at various times." For instance, she is constantly searching for a theme or a characteristic of that specific school year that she can bring to life with pictures and the context of her words.

No matter how you create and present your annual fund brochure, Kirkland says, "(an annual fund brochure) is a nice reminder, but not what makes people give. It has to have a good infrastructure behind it."

Source: Deborah Kirkland, Director of Development, The Joy School, Houston, TX. Phone (713) 523-0660. E-mail: dkirkland@thejoyschool.org. Website: www.thejoyschool.org

A page from the annual fund brochure for Joy School (Houston, TX) shows some consistent design elements used year to year, such as the schoolhouse logo as a bullet point.

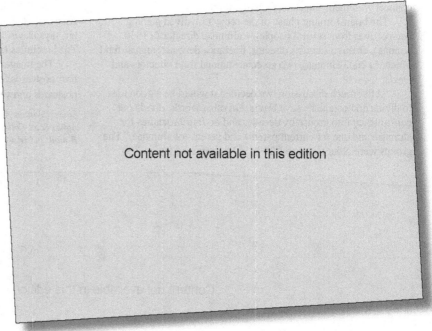

Content not available in this edition

Tips for Developing Marketing Pieces

The best marketing brochures, direct mail packages and other printed pieces are developed as a family of marketing materials that have the same look, the same theme and convey common messages, depending on the purpose of each piece.

Coming up with the most compelling messages and attention-grabbing copy can be a challenge. To prepare for writing and designing these various printed pieces, these steps will enable you to create a family of compelling and results-oriented printed communications:

1. **Collect samples.** Find out what the competition is doing. If you attend a conference, bring back samples of award-winning brochures and direct mail packages. Review those samples before you begin developing your own.

2. **Assemble compelling messages over time.** Keep a file of important achievement made by one of your organization's departments. When you come across a heartwarming story about how someone was helped by your agency, record it and file it.

3. **Collect quotes from those who have made positive comments.** Whether it's at a board meeting or a casual conversation, you no doubt hear positive comments about the work of your charity. When that occurs, ask the individual who made that statement if you can make a note of it and perhaps use it in print at some future point. Then send a note back to the individual confirming his/her approval.

4. **Focus on your mission and strategic plan.** From time to time, write out messages that underscore what your cause is all about. When it comes time to develop your communications pieces, certain messages will surface as the most attention-grabbing and convincing.

5. **What's happening in your community as a result of your agency?** Throughout the course of a year, keep an eye out for the positive ways in which your agency is impacting your community or region. Note and file those examples.

These more preparatory steps will make the job of writing marketing materials much easier and successful.

HANDOUTS, COLLATERAL MATERIALS HELP SUPPORT YOUR REQUEST

Tailor Brochures to Targeted Age Groups

Finding it difficult to appeal to different age groups in one direct mail appeal? Why not do what officials with Agnes Scott College (Decatur, GA) did with their annual fund mailings?

Agnes Scott's annual fund brochures, which won a CASE (Council for Advancement and Support of Education) award, were targeted to specific groups of alumnae.

"At an annual fund staff meeting, we were talking about how difficult it is to write a letter which appeals to all age groups," says Joanne Davis, director of annual fund. "We discussed how far apart in ages our alumnae are, from in their 90s to their early 20s, and wondered if there wasn't something different we could do to connect with them and catch their attention."

The brainstorming phase of the project involved gaining perspectives from several people — alumnae director (a 1968 alumna), creative services director, freelance designer, annual fund officer (a 2003 alumna), two associate annual fund directors and Davis.

"After much discussion, we decided it would be a good idea to divide and conquer," says Davis. "In other words, divide our constituency into groups by decades and do four brochures for alumnae and one for current parents and parents of alumnae." The groups were older alumnae ('25 to '59), alumnae ('60s to '79),

alumnae ('80 to '92), young alumnae ('93 to '03) and current students' parents and parents of graduates.

Each mailer included a photo montage featuring an age-appropriate alumna with nostalgic photos from her era and the theme, "The Power of One — The Impact of Many."

"We thought they might pay more attention to a piece that contained few words but had pictures that would evoke nostalgia and make them understand every gift is important and every gift, large or small, makes a difference," says Davis. "We wanted something that would catch their attention immediately and make them think about the college and the part it played in their life."

The college got a lot of mileage out of the brochures' theme. An e-solicitation with music and some of the same photos was a big hit, says Davis, but unfortunately, they weren't able to track results. The brochures brought in about $30,000 that they were able to track.

The images on the front of the brochures were used to make four postcards for fund chairs to write thank-you notes. Final appeal postcards and year-end, thank-you postcards were also created.

Source: Joanne A. Davis, Director of Annual Fund, Office of Development, Agnes Scott College, Decatur, GA. Phone (404) 471-5343. E-mail: jadavis@agnesscott.edu

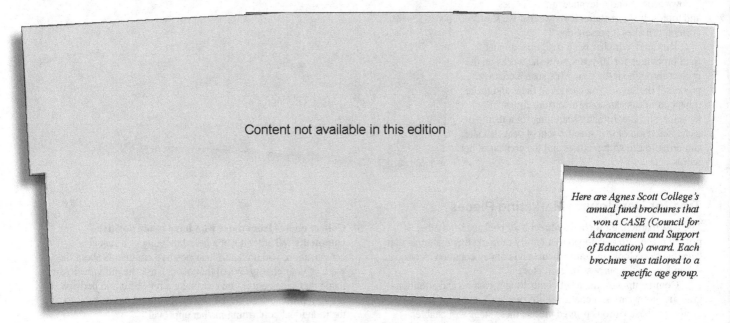

Content not available in this edition

Here are Agnes Scott College's annual fund brochures that won a CASE (Council for Advancement and Support of Education) award. Each brochure was tailored to a specific age group.

Development Brochure Ideas

Look back on the past year or two. What are your organization's top accomplishments with regard to fulfilling your mission?

Use those accomplishments as stand-out points in a brochure, then add copy under each that underscores each point — perhaps quotes from those served by your organization or a description of how that accomplishment impacts the lives of those you serve.

Why point out your accomplishments? Because people are more apt to support an organization that can demonstrate how it makes a difference in a community or region or in people's lives. People also like giving to a winner, so don't be too modest about spotlighting the headway your cause is making in fulfilling its mission.

HANDOUTS, COLLATERAL MATERIALS HELP SUPPORT YOUR REQUEST

Create a Handout Geared to Area Businesses

When calling on businesses in your community and service area, it's important to have a marketing piece that speaks directly to them and their specific organization. Printed information that could easily be tailored to business contacts includes:

✓ A list of all businesses that contributed during the past fiscal year (possibly arranged by giving clubs or levels).

✓ Messages that speak to your organization's impact on the local economy (e.g., number of employees, payroll, etc.).

✓ Brief testimonials from respected business leaders (both large and small businesses).

✓ Perks for businesses for giving at various levels.

✓ Profiles of partnerships existing between your organization and businesses.

✓ Messages about how your organization positively impacts the quality of life in your community.

✓ A separate list of businesses sponsoring various programs throughout the past year.

✓ Examples of how your organization participates as a corporate citizen (i.e., chamber member, representation on boards, etc.).

Why Give? See How Six Nonprofits Encourage Donors to Give

Looking for inspiration and fresh ideas to better connect potential givers with opportunities to give? Here are examples of how other nonprofits are finding creative ways to answer the question, "Why give?"

✓ Staff at **Dartmouth College** (Hanover, NH) determined that the cost per student per day is $300. They used that amount to illustrate on a pie chart (shown at right) where that money goes. For example, the pie chart shows that a large chunk of that $300 — $126 — is used to pay faculty who love to teach undergraduates and the staff who assist them. Learn more at: www.dartmouth.edu/~alfund/why_give/index.html

✓ **Spring Hill College** (Mobile, AL) uses quotes and photos of its college scholarship recipients and profiles of its donors to show prospective donors why it is important to give back and how they can make a difference with their gifts. See details at: www.shc.edu/giving/why-give

✓ **Texas Tech University** (Lubbock, TX) recognizes that everyone has their own reasons for making a gift, and lists some of those: "You want to return the favor;" "It's good business." For more info: www.texastech.edu/development/whygive/

✓ **MADRE** (New York, NY) shows fiscal responsibility with graphic charts showing who gives to their organization (individuals, institutional funders and others) how those donations are used. See charts at: www.madre.org/index.php?s=3&b=11

✓ **Children's Hospital Boston** (Boston, MA) shares success stories through profiles and photos of the children the hospital has helped. Check it out at: http://giving.childrenshospital.org/NetCommunity/Page.aspx?pid=225

✓ **Rainforest Action Network** (San Francisco, CA) created a video illustrating its mission and sharing success stories to encourage donors to "Become Part of the Solution." Watch the video at: http://ran.org/give/why_give/

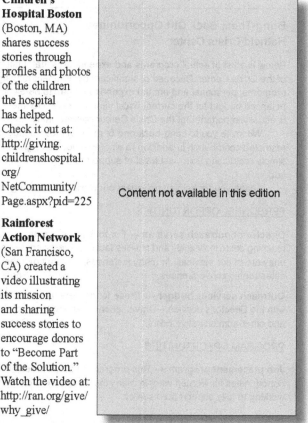

Content not available in this edition

ANNUAL GIVING IDEAS AND EXAMPLES WORTH DOING

Learn from others' successess. Here are several tried-and-tested ideas you may wish to incorporate into your own annual giving program as a way to meet and surpass yearly goals during this more turbulent economic period. Just know that you can surpass goals with the proper planning and the determination to succeed.

Last Year's Cutbacks Become This Year's Funding Opportunities

If your organization has experienced specific budget cutbacks because of the economy or other factors over which you have no control, don't overlook those items as funding opportunities for donors who want to see their gifts making a noticeable difference.

Review each budget line item or program that received the ax last year and evaluate its potential as a gift opportunity for the current year. After identifying a range of projects with varying costs, produce a bring-them-back wish list you can selectively share with individuals and businesses that may choose to fund one or more of them.

The difference between a traditional wish list and a bring-them-back list is the fact that a wish list identifies needs that have yet to be realized and a bring-them-back list identifies more crucial needs that were, until last year, part of your general operations.

It is important to point out to past contributors, however, that any gifts directed to the bring-them-back list be in addition to what they normally contribute. This, in effect, would be a way to upgrade existing donors. This obviously would not apply to previous nondonors since any gift they make would provide new money.

To the left is a sample illustration you can use as a template to create a bring-them-back wish list of your own.

Bring-Them-Back Gift Opportunities
Hatfield Crisis Center

Below is a list of actual programs and expenditures that, until this year, had been a vital part of the Crisis Center. Because of significant government funding cutbacks, however, these programs, personnel and annual expenditures had to be eliminated in order to project a balanced budget for the current fiscal year. The need for these items is imperative; however, it is equally important that the Crisis Center operate within its means.

We invite you to bring-back one or more of these budget cutback items by making a restricted contribution in addition to whatever you have given in previous years. (Unfortunately, simply redirecting your past level of support to a project would have no net impact on the budget.)

Thank you for helping us regain our footing in assisting those in need.

PERSONNEL OPPORTUNITIES

Director of outreach services — For four years, we have made a noticeable difference in reaching out to individuals and families facing domestic abuse and violence issues who were unaware of our services. In many instances, this staff member's work helped in preventing catastrophic consequences. *Replacement Cost:* *$27,000*

Outreach services budget — These funds were used to cover necessary costs associated with the Director's position — travel, phone, transportation of those in need, temporary housing and other administrative costs. *Replacement Cost:* *$12,000*

PROGRAM OPPORTUNITIES

Job placement program — This program, in place for eight years, helped find job opportunities for women who, in many instances, were on their own for the first time and working to fully support themselves. *Replacement Cost:* *$11,000*

SPECIFIC BUDGET LINE ITEMS

Hope **newsletter** — Cut back from four quarterly issues to two. Printing and postage reductions. *Replacement Cost:* *$1,100*

Facility maintenance budget — Cut back by 10 percent. *Replacement Cost:* *$840*

Professional development/training — Overall training/professional development for all personnel was cut back by 30 percent. *Replacement Cost:* *$1,500*

ANNUAL GIVING IDEAS AND EXAMPLES WORTH DOING

Beef Up Your Fundraising Budget by $50,000

Would you like to expand your fundraising efforts — add staff, purchase new computers/software, conduct more direct mail appeals — but just don't have the resources to do so? Then why not devise a plan that will do just that?

Here's one approach for beefing up your fundraising budget:

1. Quietly launch a Power of 10 campaign in which you secure 10 donors each willing to invest $5,000 over a five-year period — $1,000 per year per donor.

2. Identify as many as 50 prospects each capable of giving $5,000 over five years.

3. Looking to the most capable and committed prospects among your list of 50, assemble a five-member Power of 10 executive committee (prerequisites to membership: willingness to make a $5,000 pledge and help in approaching others to give). This group's collective commitment will amount to half your goal, $25,000.

4. Once you have this leadership group assembled, make each group responsible for approaching up to six other prospects capable of making $5,000 commitments. This is based on a 6 to1 prospect to donor ratio. In other words, each committee member may need to call on as many as six prospects to secure one $5,000 commitment.

If successful, you will have ten $5,000 commitments from this exclusive Power of 10 group. That's $10,000 per year, for five years, earmarked to expand development efforts.

When the Going Gets Tough...

Only four months into the job as its new director of development, and with no warning whatsoever, she was told: "You need to boost annual fund giving by 25 percent next year compared to this year."

Sound familiar? Happens all the time. You come into a position and, without even being consulted, are told to raise more money than ever before.

To rise to this challenge — and perhaps even exceed it —be sure to:

1. Evaluate specific fundraising strategies used in the past (e.g., phonathon, personal calls, direct mail appeals, etc.) to prioritize what has worked best and could perhaps be built upon, as well as what needs to be changed or eliminated.

2. Pay particular attention to strategies aimed at retaining and increasing the prior year's gifts. What steps can you take to invite and encourage last year's contributors to increase their level of support significantly? A special funding project? Increasing the number of personal calls?

3. Focus your attention on higher-end gifts. It's smarter to go after 25 gifts of $1,000 than to attempt to raise 1,000 gifts of $25.

4. Put it all in writing. An operational plan complete with goals, quantifiable objectives, fundraising strategies, action plans and a calendar of what needs to happen by when, will help keep you and others on course as you progress throughout the year.

Hold an Annual Fund Summit to Launch Successful Year

Exceeding previous years' annual giving is always a challenge. But that challenge can appear even more out of reach in this current economic climate and amid the added burden of budget cutbacks.

To address the challenge head-on and emerge with can-do strategies, host a day-long annual fund summit, even if you're in the middle of a fiscal year. Invite your key stakeholders — development staff and other key employees, board members, development committee, top annual fund supporters in previous years and others — to find solutions.

Utilize the annual fund summit to:

1. **Draw participants' attention to the dilemma facing your nonprofit.** Spell out what will happen to programs and to those you serve if your goal is not met.

2. **Summarize previous year's fundraising strategies** (e.g. direct mail, phonathon, personal calls, gift club strategies), including how much was raised with each effort.

3. **Share obstacles to success.** Make mention of how any budget cutbacks to your development operation may impede your efforts.

4. **Share your current plan of action to meet this year's annual fund goal.** Point out obstacles you may face with particular fundraising strategies sharing possible solutions to each dilemma.

5. **Devote time to brainstorming.** Using a facilitator, spend time asking participants to offer new or improved ideas for meeting and surpassing your goal.

6. **Create a revised action plan.** Once ample time has been given to brainstorming, ask the group to prioritize their collective ideas. Hopefully, many of the ideas generated will require their ongoing participation in identifying, cultivating and soliciting gifts and sponsorships throughout the year.

By engaging these key stakeholders, you will not only enlist their help in a variety of ways, you will also motivate them to give as generously as possible during this challenging time, and encourage those within their respective circles of influence to do the same.

ANNUAL GIVING IDEAS AND EXAMPLES WORTH DOING

Grateful Patient Program Builds on What Patients Want to Hear and What They Don't

At Huntsville Hospital Foundation (Huntsville, AL), development officers Susan Ready and Emily Miller recently boosted grateful donor response from zero to $16,762 in the effort's six months.

The new program, Honoring Care Champions is built on these tenets:

❑ **Allow the patient to say thanks to someone special.** By making a gift, Huntsville's grateful patients are able to honor a service employee of their choice (doctor, nurse, orderly, etc.) as a Huntsville Hospital Care Champion. The foundation's COO publicly presents that employee with a silver, engraved pin and a card with the personalized message from the patient.

❑ **Get the word out.** Ready and Miller began their campaign by first presenting to their board, department heads, front-line managers and staff. They included information about the program in the employee newsletter and websites for the hospital, foundation and staff. Additionally, they advertised the program via a brochure; a letter from the foundation president calling new grateful patients to action; flier in patient packets; posters throughout the hospital and postcards mailed to patients 90 days after discharge, emphasizing a consistent message throughout.

❑ **Let patient determine gift size,** perpetuating the message that "every little bit helps." Gifts range from $5 to $3,000.

❑ **Low cost.** Since January, the program has honored 300-plus hospital employees on behalf of 200-plus patients, many of whom are first-time donors, with gross revenue of $16,762 outweighing initial printing and mailing costs.

❑ **Asking the right patients.** Ready and Miller are still refining their system; they do not solicit patients who are uninsured or on government assistance, but have not yet tapped all possible populations of patients such as new mothers in the maternity ward.

Sources: Susan Ready, Director of Annual Giving; Emily Miller, Manager of Donor Relations; Huntsville Hospital Foundation, Huntsville, AL. Phone (256) 265-8077. E-mail: susan.ready@hhsys. org or emily.miller@hhsys.org

---

A Delicate Balance: What Grateful Patients Don't Want to Hear

Before Susan Ready and Emily Miller took over the grateful patient program at Huntsville Hospital Foundation (Huntsville, AL), their organization had to learn the hard way what didn't work in the tricky business of turning grateful patients into donors.

Here are some pitfalls to avoid:

1. **Letters from the top.** Huntsville's old program informed potential grateful patients about the program via a letter from the CEO. Patients did not respond to the CEO because he was the one signing the bill.

2. **Letters from a peer.** For a personal approach, former development officers sent a letter conceived and signed by a past patient, who was a million-dollar donor. Miller explains, "It looked like our grateful patient was sitting at home with a patient list. Even though it wasn't true, it sent the wrong message."

3. **Information without a call to action.** Development officers sent a brochure which told the million-dollar donor's story, showed his photo, even included a testimonial from his son. But they didn't include a letter asking for support. With no call to action, the piece looked like an advertisement for the hospital.

Content not available in this edition

ANNUAL GIVING IDEAS AND EXAMPLES WORTH DOING

Consider a Three-year (Increasing Gift) Pledge

Rather than meeting every year with a donor for a $500 gift, try this approach: Meet with the donor and invite a $2,250 pledge to be paid over a three-year period: $500 in year one; $750 in year two and $1,000 in year three.

If successful, you will be relatively assured of continued support for three years rather than one. Plus, you will have secured increased giving during that period. And securing the three-year pledge frees you up to focus more on approaching new donors.

If you do use this multi-year approach to increase giving among current donors however, it's crucial that you continue to stay in touch with those loyal supporters.

Annual Giving Strategies: Offer More Restricted Gifts

Although the pressure is on to raise more unrestricted gifts during tough economic times, you may actually have greater success marketing restricted gifts — those that fund specific programs or projects.

Why?

Because would-be contributors are more likely to support those funding projects that interest them. They don't want to think their gifts are going into some big black hole.

In addition to soliciting unrestricted gifts supporting general operations (e.g., scholarships, patient care, client services), carry out targeted asks that include restricted gift options.

You may share a wish list of restricted gift opportunities with non-donors, for example. Or later in your fiscal year you may ask those who have already made an unrestricted gift to consider a second gift restricted to a project of their choosing.

2020 Is Magic Number for Girls Inc. Annual Campaign

After hosting a huge annual luncheon for 20 years at the expense of an annual campaign, supporters of Girls Inc. of Metropolitan Dallas (Dallas, TX) decided to try something new.

The annual luncheon was a monster, says Lisa Shay, chief development officer. "The work associated with it prevented us from doing an annual campaign." So this year, their board of trustees decided to cancel the luncheon and create the Girls Inc. 2020 Fund.

Shay says $2,020 is the cost for a full year of programs and support for one girl.

"There was some talk of making it an even $2,000," she says, "but we thought it was important to attach the actual cost to the donation to make it real for people."

Since the campaign began in September 2008, they have received 250 donations totaling more than $196,000. Of that:

✓ 49 percent of existing donors have increased their giving.

✓ 12 donors have given at the full sponsorship level of $2,020.

✓ Three donors have given $10,000.

✓ Three other donors have sponsored two girls each at a total gift of $4,040

Most telling though, says Shay, are the 84 donors who gave an amount equaling the actual cost of supplying a specific program or service to a Girls Inc. member, which she says "shows that people are really connecting to the idea behind the campaign."

Shay attributes the campaign's success largely to the follow-through of campaign cabinet members who called donors to set up face-to-face meetings and ask for gifts.

In addition Shay says, "I think people are ready for a little more transparency in their donations. The 2020 Fund puts the focus back on the girls. They're not just giving $200 to become a Bronze Circle member. They are being given the opportunity to truly impact the life of a girl."

Source: Lisa Shay, Chief Development Officer, Girls Inc. of Metropolitan Dallas, Dallas, TX. Phone (214) 654-4530. E-mail: lshay@girlincdallas.org

A fact sheet explains the 2020 Fund for Girls Incorporated of Metropolitan Dallas (Dallas, TX).

Content not available in this edition

ANNUAL GIVING IDEAS AND EXAMPLES WORTH DOING

Raise $50,000 More in Annual Gifts

Need an extra $50,000 in annual gift revenue? You can do it by building a set of action plans centered around one strategy. The key is picking a strategy best suited for your organization and sticking to it.

All too many nonprofits spread themselves too thin by doing a little more in direct mail, a little more in phonathons, a little more in face-to-face calls, etc. Instead, zero in on one fundraising strategy that makes sense for your organization and then build a set of sub-strategies around it.

To the right are three examples of key strategy options broken down into sub-strategies that help illustrate this approach.

**Three Focused Strategy Options
To Generate $50,000 in New Gift Revenue**

Option No. 1: **Longfellow Society (Annual Gifts of $1,000 or more)
Generate 50 New Members**

Member-recruit-a-member Initiative ....Goal:	$20,000
Staff Calls (four new members per staff member) ....Goal:	$16,000
Targeted Direct Mail Appeal ....Goal:	$10,000
Board Development Committee ....Goal:	$10,000

Option No. 2: **New Sponsorships (To Underwrite Programs/Services)**

Wellness Initiative...Goal:	$20,000
Outreach/Mobile Unit ....Goal:	$10,000
Neonatal..Goal:	$20,000

Option No. 3: New Special Events

September Western-themed outdoor fundraiser ....Goal:	$15,000
December Tour of Homes ....Goal:	$18,000
April Fashion Show ....Goal:	$8,000
May Golf/Tennis Classic ....Goal:	$20,000

Committee of 100 Generates $50,000

Want to generate more $500 gifts for your annual fund? Here's one idea:

1. Initiate an exclusive annual gift club for anyone willing to make an annual contribution of $500 and give it a name such as The Committee of 100.

2. Anyone who gives at that level gets the privilege of voting how they wish to have their donations used based on recommendations from staff. Committee members choose how they wish their donations to be spent.

3. To increase membership in your Committee of 100, send an appeal directed to a targeted group of would-be donors and/ or coordinate a phonathon. In addition, host special receptions for key individuals in your community or targeted areas that includes a brief program outlining the committee's goals.

If successful, your Committee of 100 will result in $50,000 in gifts directed to a funding project (or projects) that the group has collectively chosen.

Multiple-year Giving Society Surprises With First-year Success

If your organization relies significantly on grants, know that your slice of that pie may narrow as needs of the aging baby boomer generation place more demands on such funds.

Instead, consider replacing some of those funds with a multiple year giving society.

Annie K. Eveleigh, director of development, Senior Resources, Inc. (Columbia, SC), says her board of directors was looking to identify funding sources other than grants for this very reason. So she brought the idea of a multiple-year giving society to the table.

Eveleigh used a multiple-year fundraising plan as a model for the organization's Every Senior Counts Multiple Year Giving Society. She, her staff and board spent several years researching organizations that used the model, creating a community awareness plan, purchasing a donor data base system and forming a steering committee.

In July 2007, organization staff began offering public tours to give an inside look of its programs through photos, stories and testimonials. Eveleigh says they were careful to not make the tours fundraisers, but did invite participants to the giving society kickoff.

The kickoff featured a fundraising breakfast in November 2007. Twenty-four table captains — community leaders, volunteers and board members — invited friends, colleagues and family, drawing 220 guests to the complimentary breakfast.

After hearing moving client testimonials, guests were given pledge cards and asked to pledge $1,000, $5,000 or $10,000 per year for five years. Many pledged for the entire five years, some for two or three and others gave a one-time donation, says Eveleigh. She notes they had a goal of raising $40,000 and ended up raising almost $221,000.

Eveleigh and staff called each pledge to say thank-you and get feedback on the event.

Source: Annie K. Eveleigh, Director of Development, Senior Resources, Columbia, SC. Phone (803) 252-7734.
E-mail: seniorresourcesinc@sc.rr.com

ANNUAL GIVING IDEAS AND EXAMPLES WORTH DOING

Analyze Your Mailing List at Least Annually

When was the last time you reviewed your database to determine who is and who is not contributing on an annual basis?

Should your list be expanded or pruned? Do you have solicitation strategies aimed at specific list segments?

Analyzing your list and developing strategies aimed at increasing the overall percentage of annual contributors is well worth the time and effort involved.

To fine-tune your mailing list, conduct these exercises:

- Determine the existing percentage of those who contributed last year and set a challenging percentage increase as next year's goal. Quantifying what you hope to achieve commits you to developing a plan to meet that goal.

- Identify your list's lybunts (those who gave last year but not this) and sybunts (those who give some years but not this) and develop specific strategies to secure their gifts. These groups should more readily make contributions.

- Evaluate the demographics of your non-donors (age, gender, location and more) to determine targeted strategies. For example, you may want to solicit prospects geographically for projects that will benefit their communities or regions. Or, perhaps you will want to develop funding projects based on the age ranges within your constituency.

- Evaluate your system of donor benefits and incentives. Should changes be made?

- Share your list of non-donors with board members, your development committee or other key volunteers, and develop a plan that encourages them to help solicit particular persons or businesses.

Y'ALL Campaign Reaches Out to Young Alumni

Development staff at the University of South Carolina (Columbia, SC) created a young alumni program to instill the importance of philanthropy in recent graduates.

Steve Farwick, assistant director of annual giving, answers questions about the Face of Y'ALL (Young Alumni Leaving a Legacy) campaign:

Please describe the Face of Y'ALL program.

"We launched the Face of Y'ALL, a first-of-its-kind campaign targeted toward Columbia campus graduates of the last decade, (in early 2008). Young alumni are the future of the university, after all, and Carolina wants graduates' voices to be heard, while also helping classes of the last 10 years leave a legacy at their alma mater.

"We've discovered many recent graduates don't fully understand that tuition and state assistance are not fully covering the cost of an education. We want them to be aware of the fact that a considerable number of alumni and friends were passionate about supporting their education.

"A 12 percent campaign response rate exceeded our expectations for the Face of Y'ALL.... Nearly 1,600 recent alumni submitted updated biographical information, 139 applied to be the Face of Y'ALL and almost 1,000 voted for their favorite once the pool was narrowed down to five by a university committee. Once all the votes were tallied we ended with two fantastic representatives for our young alumni base."

What role have these faces played? What activities have they been involved in?

"Our two winners, Joey and Emily, are invited to the president's pre-game parties, given special privileges at football games, enjoyed a shopping spree at the university bookstore and are VIP guests at receptions and other university events. Most importantly, Joey and Emily are assisting with the creation of a Young Alumni Advancement Council (that) will help graduates of the last decade become better educated about the importance of philanthropy, share the university's mission with peers, promote participation and select marketing materials for their constituency. Joey and Emily will co-chair the council."

From a development standpoint, why was the campaign started?

"To help create philanthropic awareness and encourage participation in giving among our most recent graduates. Too often, universities focus on alumni who meet certain gift levels or other qualifications. We saw a great opportunity, despite a lower short-term return on investment, with our newest alumni. Educating them now through the Web, e-mail, direct mail and call center is paying off in huge dividends. The Y'ALL campaign has allowed us to communicate with this age group as we wouldn't other alumni constituencies. Why does Carolina need their support? Is participation really more important than dollar amount given? Collectively, how can recent graduates make a difference? These are just some of the topics we address throughout the entire campaign. It's pivotal that these young alumni know they are the future of their alma mater in more ways than one."

Content not available in this edition

What are the goals of the Y'ALL campaign?

"Engaging graduates of the last decade, educating them about the important role they play as alumni donors, having them serve on volunteer boards, carrying the university's momentum across the nation, serving their alma mater with pride and ensuring young alumni stay connected to Carolina. As we continue the program, we create even more awareness about philanthropy and the university as a whole. Since launching the campaign, the number of donors from the young alumni segment has increased by 16 percent. So far this fiscal year, the majority of all online gifts are from this particular group as well."

Source: Steve Farwick, Assistant Director of Annual Giving Programs, University of South Carolina, Columbia, SC. Phone (803) 777-2592. E-mail: sfarwick@mailbox.sc.edu

ANNUAL GIVING IDEAS AND EXAMPLES WORTH DOING

You Can't Afford to NOT Raise Funds in a Down Economy

The recent economic crisis may have some nonprofit leaders putting fundraising plans on hold because they believe now is not the right time to ask people for money. But that's the worst thing to do, says Tony Poderis, author of "It's A Great Day to Fund Raise!"

"In far too many nonprofits, there is an initial rush, when the going gets tough, to cut services and staff rather than have the respective boards of trustees pitch in and work even harder," says Poderis. "It is far too easy to give up (on fundraising goals)."

While now may be a difficult time to raise funds, that shouldn't stop you from trying, says Poderis. Here's why:

- **Out of sight, out of mind.** Taking a break in fundraising can be like giving your donors away. "Other nonprofits won't have waited," he says. "They'll have solicited your donors."

- **A campaign deferred is a campaign defeated.** Poderis says ramifications can be long lasting, including loss of volunteers,

rescinded pledges and donors who have already committed wondering what will happen to their gifts. Media might even use the deferred or suspended campaign to suggest the organization is in trouble.

- **Assuming donor intent.** If you don't ask, you'll never know. "Never take it upon yourself to determine what donors will or will not do," Poderis says. "That's their privilege." He suggests giving donors options and letting them choose.

Even with the current economic realities, Poderis says his experience as a fundraising consultant suggests that many people still have money to give to their favorite causes: "Some are able to give more than others and some may be able to give less than they have previously, but most still have something to give."

Source: Tony Poderis, Fundraising Consultant, Willoughby Hills, OH. E-mail: tony@raise-funds.com

Make Your Case for Support in Hard Economic Times

Statistics show direct correlations between struggling economies and struggling families. That can mean an increase in demand for services of nonprofit organizations that help meet needs of such families, including food banks, homeless shelters and even domestic violence shelters.

For organizations having such a direct connection to the current economic downturn, making a clear case for continued or additional support is fairly straightforward.

But what if your organization doesn't have a direct connection? You need to find one to make a case for support in tough times.

Use this opportunity to identify how your organization might be affected by the current economy and offer supporters the chance to help you with their gifts.

For example, your animal shelter might see an increase in surrendered pets because people can't afford to care for them anymore. If you provide clothing to low-income women for job interviews you might see a decrease in the amount of clothing donations because people can't afford to buy new clothes and

give you their old ones. Making a case for why support of your organization is still as important as it was before the souring of the economy is imperative in helping to keep your organization on people's short list for donations.

Following the terrorist attacks of Sept. 11, 2001, officials with the Make-A-Wish Foundation of America reinforced the message that families of children with life-threatening medical conditions continued to struggle with uncertainty every day. The children's illnesses and the ordeals they faced with treatments and long hospital stays didn't change because of 9/11, but the need to provide those children with hope by granting their heartfelt wishes was still there.

During the next year, the foundation's direct mail pieces told the stories of children whose wishes had been inspired by the events of 9/11, including a girl who asked to deliver guardian angel pins to firefighters in New York City.

Source: Brent Goodrich, Media Relations Manager, Make-A-Wish Foundation of America, Phoenix, AZ. Phone (602) 279-9474. E-mail: bgoodrich@wish.org